THE ARCHITECT
LOVE

YOUR PERFECT RELATIONSHIP STARTS HERE

AR'NIE ROZAH KROGH

THE ARCHITECT OF LOVE

First published in Great Britain 2017
Published by 7th Tribe Publishing

Copyright © 2017 Ar'nie Rozah Krogh

All rights reserved. No part of this publication may be reproduced, stored in or introduced into a retrieval system, or transmitted, in any form, or by any means (electronic, mechanical, photocopying, recording or otherwise) without the prior written permission of the publisher.

> **The names and circumstances of clients and other identifying characteristics in case histories have been changed to protect their privacy.**

This book is sold subject to the condition that it shall not, by way of trade or otherwise, be lent, resold, hired out, or otherwise circulated without the publisher's prior consent in any form of binding or cover other than that in which it is published and without a similar condition including this condition being imposed on the subsequent purchaser.

ISBN 978-0-9957997-0-7

Editorial Assistance by The Write Factor
"Love" concept design by Dorte Good
Cover & page design by Lisa Hall @ Lemonberry.com
Chapter illustrations by Laxmi Hussein

Dedication

To the person who made this book possible. To the man who kept it all together when I was breaking apart. To the man who taught me to ask the tough questions in life. To the man possibly sent from the heavens above, my husband,
Anders Krogh.

Acknowledgement

As everyone knows, no author can write a well-written book without the help of others. Even though I have always loved writing in school and continued blogging as an adult, I am no journalist. I needed lots of encouragement and a little help along the way.

To my 3 star supporters, thank you for believing in me: Mike German (my chaperone during my dates with hubby), Steffen Boelaars (he has taken some amazing photos of me and helped sort out my sticky Apple issues in the past) and Nisa Khan (a Media student, turned soul sister, whom I met in London for an interview, making me determined to learn more about sharing knowledge). Your strong belief in my success has helped me get through the rough patch when nearing the end of this book. Thank you to Rob, Lorna and Emily of The Write Factor for the editorial assistance and the hours of explaining to me how a book should be, what is well written and what needs improving. Thank you too to designer Lisa Hall for your enthusiasm in this project and being patient with me. Gratitude also to Deborah Valentine for giving me a great insight for my blurb at such short notice.

To the many members of my International Mixed Marriages group I started in 2007, you all have been instrumental in showing to me what a relationship/marriage/union is all about. Thank you too to those who have poured your heart and soul to me over these years. I have learnt so much from you.

I am also thankful to the au pairs and babysitters who've come into our lives and helped me be a better mum and professional by picking up my slack when the ideas are flowing.

An acknowledgement will not be complete without a nod to my dearest family and close friends. To my eldest sister Siti aka Lili and my first 'baby', niece Hartini, thank you for always getting my back and being there for me through good times and bad times. To my mum, who is a central figure in my releasing this book, I hope I have done you proud as a single mum, even though I was not the easiest of a child.

Of course, my own nucleus family deserves to be acknowledged. My 4 children for being patient when mummy needed to write and is lost in her own world. To my 3 girls, Adeena Maia Krogh, Amelia Zara Krogh and Arièna Ayla Krogh, I'm so proud of you for being such kind yet strong girls and to my son, Asger Seif Krogh, I am so glad that you've learnt to respect and love women at such a tender age. My husband who helped cook, clean and picked the pieces I dropped and teaching our kids what is love and joy. You're all my inspiration to keep the love going for others.

Lastly, to all the bloggers and writers out there, thank you for sharing your knowledge with us. Thank you to my online community for being my cheerleaders. To those I've missed mentioning yet have played a part on my professional journey, thank you. I heart you all.

CONTENTS

Dedication..iii
Acknowledgement...iv
Introduction The Road To Happiness Starts Here............ix

Chapters

1. The Exterior Of Your House..1
2. The Layout Of Your House..35
3. How You Furnish Your House...................................67
4. Knowing What You Want...99
5. The Bedrock To Happiness..129
6. Everything In The Garden Is Rosy............................163
7. Road Blocks & Speedbumps.....................................193
Love Is Just Around The Corner...................................215
The 20 Questions Game...217
Bibliography..220
About the Author..223

INTRODUCTION

THE ROAD TO HAPPINESS STARTS HERE

You've bought this book because you want to find 'the one' – am I right? Well, I'm happy to say that this is a dream that can come true, and I'm here to help you achieve it. The secrets that I will reveal to you in this book are not rocket science, they don't require a PhD to put into action – what I'm going to tell you is more about commonsense, about applying yourself to the task with confidence and a clear vision of exactly what it is that you want. I can hear you thinking: "If it's so easy, why haven't I succeeded before?" Well, you'd be surprised just how many of us forget the basics when we approach the complex issue of our love lives. It seems to me that very often, all rational thinking goes out of the window – and then we end up wondering what went wrong! But the good news is that within you lies the ability to achieve lasting happiness, and I will help you unlock that potential. Prepare for happiness, because love is coming your way!

> *Everyone deserves happiness and has within them the ability to find it*

You are the architect of your own love life, and within these pages you will learn how to design and build the perfect relationship. There's actually no magic formula that you can apply: instead, I'm going to ask you to do a bit of honest self-assessment and soul-searching, so that you can learn how to trust in yourself – your gut instinct – about what it is that makes you happy. Believe me when I say that you already have within you, all the tools you'll ever need to succeed. In just a few short chapters, you will be equipped with your new-found knowledge, and you can go out and discover a whole new world of possibilities.

    I chose the analogy of becoming an 'architect of love' because it's a solid, concrete (pun intended) way to visualise your future. The concept of love is rather abstract, and having a clear metaphor of a house gives you an easy way to understand what you need to do to allow love to enter your life. In the same way that a house can't be built overnight, but requires careful planning and preparation concerning the structure, the layout, the rooms and the setting, so too do you need to examine your soul, your personality, your preferences and needs, in order to give you the best chance of success.

    In the following chapters, I invite you to imagine building the home that you've always wanted and then use that as a metaphorical template for the relationship you've always wanted. In its most basic sense this means, for example, reflecting on how the need for good foundations in a house are essential in a relationship too. The symbolism of 'home' also contains within it the implicit 'happily ever after' connotation that home has to most of us – after all, at the end of all good fairy tales, the blissful couple set up home together, whether it's in a castle or a cottage. In the same way, by the end of this book, you will have envisaged your perfect home, from the foundations to the furnishings, the layout to the location, and by doing this, you'll be primed and ready for love. Your intention to create the right relationship will reverberate as an irresistible energy that the universe will respond to. You just have to be aware enough to recognise when your wish has come true!

INTRODUCTION - THE ROAD TO HAPPINESS STARTS HERE

> *It's just a matter of becoming open to 'possibility'*

I wrote this book partly for all my single friends who have been nagging me for advice about finding love – here it is, guys and girls! – but I also want to reach out to everyone, regardless of gender, sexuality, age or culture, who is struggling to find their soulmate, because everyone deserves happiness and has within them the ability to find it. It's just a matter of becoming open to the possibility.

So, what makes me the right person to write this book? Although my experience as a life coach has taught me a great deal about relationships, and my training as a Master Practitioner in Neuro-Linguistic Programming has equipped me with the skills to teach communication and visualisation, my main inspiration has been my own life. My early years were a roller-coaster of a ride, starting in Singapore, where I saw my parents' rocky marriage disintegrate, leaving my mum penniless and alone. I learnt a lot about resilience from her, as well as my grandmother, who was a strong and admirable woman, a mother to the whole community. I then spread my wings and flew around the world, studying and working in many different countries. My eyes were opened to different cultures and I became much more receptive to new experiences and ways of thinking. I threw myself into this glittering international treasure trove and realised that I was truly happy as a global nomad, comfortable in many different cultures and with many different people.

> *Join me in the best adventure of your life!*

THE ARCHITECT OF LOVE

I had my own fair share of heartache (which I'll go into more fully in the book) before meeting Anders, the love of my life and my soulmate. We have four beautiful children together – and through them I have learnt the challenging lessons of parenting, of remaining true to yourself even whilst all around you are clamouring for attention.

All the love I have received from them has encouraged me to pursue my mission: by writing this book I want to spread more love and kindness in this world. I want to see more people happy within themselves and sharing their happiness with the people around them. What I want to achieve I know cannot be done by just little old me. I need you to help me. Together, we will form an army of love. So let's start at the beginning. Turn over the page and join me in the best adventure of your life.

CHAPTER ONE

THE EXTERIOR OF YOUR HOUSE

THE EXTERIOR OF YOUR HOUSE

FIRST IMPRESSIONS COUNT

What's the first thing you look at on an estate agent's property details? The photograph. You fall in love with how a house looks, rather than whether it's got a utility room or an en-suite in the guest bedroom. Similarly, when you meet someone new, rightly or wrongly, the primary focus is on appearance rather than political preferences or shoe size. It's true to say that we still 'judge a book by its cover'. Similarly, we don't consider personality first, we primarily form our opinions of people based on how they look, assuming that we will get to know them later. But, if we don't like how someone looks, we often don't bother to get to know them. That's a harsh but fair evaluation of the dating scene.

Now you might think, "Well, that's their loss. How shallow." But is it really their loss? Perhaps it's yours. Think about it: if you went for a walk and came across a shop with dirty windows, peeling paint on the door and an 'Open' sign that was swinging loose, would you really want to go in, even if inside, the shop was an Aladdin's cave of delights?

You might have heard that it takes about 30 seconds for us to judge people by the way they look – but think again. 30 seconds is a veritable *ice age* according to research by Princeton psychologists Janine Willis and Alexander Todorov[1]. They say that it only takes a tenth of a second to draw up a whole laundry list of assumptions about someone, literally in the blink of an eye, based on what you look like – your clothes, hairstyle, smile, how you carry yourself and the rest of your nonverbal communication. These all have a huge impact on how you come across to others. And guess what? Those instantaneous judgments don't change significantly even when you have more time to consider your decision. Appearances do count. Just like when you're walking down the road trying to find a certain house you'd like to buy, and you judge each property on the way in terms of how they look: "Oh, that one has a smart front door," or, "I like those fancy house numbers," and "Nice window boxes!" As you walk past, every little detail goes towards your overall opinion of the area. And how your heart sinks when you arrive at your destination and it turns out to be the scruffy one of the row!

> *It only takes a tenth of a second to draw up a whole laundry list of assumptions about someone*

These judgments can also be lasting ones; psychologists call it the 'halo effect', which describes how someone's overall impression of you influences how they feel about you. I think this is a really good analogy and an easy one to remember: so when you first meet someone, remember the halo of light and friendliness that emanates from you at that time will be what people remember – and similarly, if you're in a fug, feeling really grumpy and unforthcoming, that's what they'll remember too. The halo effect means that, if you meet someone and they decide that you're a good person, then they'll assume that everything you do will be exceptional. This explains why advertisers are so keen to use beautiful actors to promote their products: because we already admire George Clooney and Scarlett Johansson, we assume that they know about coffee and perfume and that what they recommend will be as shiny and lovely as they are.

THE EXTERIOR OF YOUR HOUSE

It's scary how all-encompassing the assumptions people make are, based purely on first impressions. It's not just, "Gosh, they're attractive!" – it goes far deeper than that. The simple fact of how you look has an impact on what they think your educational level is, how successful and competent you are at your job, your social standing, how trustworthy you are, what type of personality you have and even what your sense of humour is like. Obviously, they can't actually *know* whether these perceptions are accurate, but it's better to send out the right messages, rather than scurry around after everyone saying, "I know I *look* like a complete mess, but actually I'm very together and organised." If you want people to regard you positively, then you have to put your best self forward.

It brings to mind a dear friend of mine who is one of the nicest people you could ever wish to meet – and yet she still hasn't found her soulmate. In the most tactful of ways I've tried to raise the issue of her personal dress code, or more accurately, the fact that she doesn't have one. She's eternally in jeans, trainers and a baggy jumper, but doesn't seem to realise that's not appropriate attire for a date. She rarely has her hair cut and so it's long, lank and lifeless, and she has never tried to wear a smidgen of make-up. Now, I totally respect that how she dresses is her decision, yet just like the shop window that doesn't display the goods inside to best effect, so my friend isn't making the most of her considerable assets: her beautiful eyes, her auburn hair and her hourglass figure.

> *If you want people to regard you positively, then you have to put your best self forward*

I'm a firm believer in the law of attraction – the theory that like attracts like – so if you present the very best 'you' to the world, you'll be sure to attract your very best partner. To return to the house analogy again – your home may be humble, it may not have fifteen bedrooms and a swimming pool, but there's someone out there who will think it's their dream house. One couple I worked with reminded me how true this is:

THE EXTERIOR OF YOUR HOUSE

Sports Day, Every Day

Vicky and Ian are both of medium height and average appearance, not particularly exceptional to look at, some might say, but what gives them that extra 'edge' is that they are very physically fit – the kind of people who you might consider to be 'gym rats'. They both agree that being fit is a very attractive attribute, perhaps the most attractive, in their eyes. Toned muscles, a healthy glow, the extra energy that comes from regular exercise, they both had it by the bucket-load, and once they'd identified their shared love of working out, they gravitated towards one another like moths to a flame. They recognise in each other something they are proud of about themselves, and this constantly reinforces their positive feelings for each other. They encourage each other to go to the gym and again this ensures that the reason for their initial attraction continues to flourish.

I asked them what would happen if one of them lost that 'fit' look, or if ill health or some other reason turned them from trim to flabby. "I don't think it would affect our love for each other," mused Ian, "though it could affect our relationship in other ways..." I probed a little deeper here to find out what he meant, and Vicky replied, "I would like to think that after the two years we've been together, our love is now deeper than just how we look, or how attractive we find each other, but going to the gym together is a really important part of our lives and motivates us to have a healthy lifestyle. If one of us became ill or couldn't work out for some reason, I'd like to think that we would find another way to keep fit and healthy, like swimming or walking." Ian agreed, going so far as to say that maybe they should get a dog!

To me, this goes to show how important it is to continue making an effort, not just in staying attractive to your partner, but having the flexibility to find ways of being together and sharing interests that bring both partners enjoyment – whether it's the first flush of the relationship, or many years down the line.

If you want to keep your soulmate devoted to you, then you need to appeal to them in their own particular way, focusing not just on what you want, but what you know that they want too. It has been said that a relationship should be a competition in generosity, so if you make an effort to please your partner, this will be reciprocated, and they will endeavour to do what pleases you too. What comes around really does go around, and this becomes a virtuous circle of love, gratitude and enjoyment of the time spent with each other.

Thankfully, Vicky and Ian are still motivating each other to stay physically fit and healthy. Their story serves to remind us that you don't have to be 'beautiful' to find love, just beautiful in your partner's eyes.

The Attraction of Mindfulness

Now, if you want to be an architect of love, then in the same way that you would make sure that your house is spick and span, complete with artfully arranged flowers and bowls of fruit dotted around before you put it on the market, you need to ensure that you're doing the utmost to present yourself favourably for the best chance to meet a soulmate. When viewing a potential home, you're much more likely to 'ooh and aah' over a pile of soft, fluffy throws and cushions than a tidemark around the bath and a pile of unwashed plates, now aren't you! So make scrubbing yourself up until you're presentable a priority. To my mind, there is something attractive and appealing about almost everyone I meet, and it's vital that you discover what your best assets are, and make the most of them so they shine out as soon as someone looks at you – and I'm not just talking about your six-pack or your hour-glass figure here. To me, a generous smile is the very best facelift – and it can light up a room. And it's said that, 'the eyes are a window to the soul,' so let your eyes shine, and dazzle all who meet you. Yes, it's true that what's inside is important, and we'll be looking at that in much more detail in Chapter 2, but believe me, to make the best first impression, don't underestimate the fact that how you look plays a big part.

This explains why as a society, we spend so much money attempting to look our best. For example, in America, in 2008, over $200bn was spent on products and services that aim to improve our physical appearance, despite the country going through a recession at that time. At first this was explained as, 'the lipstick effect' – that is, the idea that during times of financial hardship, women are more likely to splash out on cosmetics to boost their attractiveness in the hope of meeting a solvent partner. However, Professor Margaret Neale of Stanford University[2] suggests a different theory, and one that recognises how men are also becoming much more likely to spend money on their physical appearance. She says that both men and women care about their physical appearance because it's linked to social status, specifically, *our perception of our own social status*. In her study, she discovered that if you *think* you are physically attractive, then you believe that you belong to a higher social strata, regardless of whether you are actually drop-dead gorgeous or have been invited to the Queen's garden party.

I find this an interesting study because it goes on to say that if we believe we're of a higher status we feel more confident, which in itself is attractive. Conversely, some people may behave more egotistically and less generously, putting themselves before others and using others for personal gain, which is obviously not a great thing. So, I'm interested in how we can find a balance between feeling good about our appearance and not behaving selfishly, and what I find to be the key to this conundrum – and it has to be said, to most others in life – is being *mindful* of the way we behave. We need to become more self-aware, and question the motives behind our behaviour, making sure that we always consider other people's feelings and that we are acting with compassion and good intent.

Mindfulness is on trend right now – and celebrities are vouching for its virtues, but what mindfulness is really all about, in essence, is being self-aware: taking one step away from your ego and personality and just watching what it is that makes you tick. When you act with mindfulness, you are more likely to act with compassion and kindness and that is the most attractive thing of all. So, it is possible to feel attractive and behave attractively!

> *A generous smile is the very best facelift*

Why does it matter so much how attractive you feel? Professor Neale explains that it's because in society, there are lots of advantages to being found attractive. For example, if you're attractive you are more likely to be successful at interviews, command a bigger salary and be promoted. A University of Texas study of MBA graduates, in 2011[3], found a 10-15% difference in earnings between the most and least attractive people in a group – adding up to a loss of earnings of thousands of dollars over a lifetime. If you're perceived as unattractive, then you're judged to be less competent and less approachable than your glossy counterparts. So when we're agonising over what outfit to wear and fretting about having a bad hair day, it's not because we're vain or insecure, it's because we know that looking good helps us to climb up the ladder of success.

If this has made you feel anxious about elements of your appearance that you can't do anything about, such as a rather large nose or a receding hairline, don't despair. There are some lovely social scientists working hard to reassure you. Firstly, psychologist Dr Emily Lovegrove[4] (great name!), says that there are downsides to being drop-dead gorgeous. In the workplace, there can be subconscious 'lookism' during the recruitment process, because very attractive women are thought to be both a distraction to lustful colleagues and less loyal than their plainer cohorts. "It is thought that attractive women don't have staying power, partly because with their looks they could go anywhere," says Dr Lovegrove, who was interviewed in *The*

Telegraph newspaper. "We are easily intimidated by those we perceive to be more beautiful than us. For instance, if you are a woman, you might not want to give a job to a much younger, more attractive woman who you worry may overtake you in the workplace." Men too, suffer for their good looks. They're less likely to get a job in a competitive field such as banking or sales if the interviewer is less attractive than them, as they're seen as a threat.

And outside the workplace, the outlook is sunnier too. Dating website OKCupid reported that people who were judged to be fair-to-middling in attractiveness but who had a quirky photo and an appealing profile received more messages than obvious stunners[5]. This is because if someone is ranked very highly, people become intimidated, whereas someone with a more average ranking is seen as being attainable.

So now you're comforted that you don't have to struggle with the burden that is exquisite beauty, let's focus on what you can do to attract interest.

The Feel Good Factor

It's much easier than you think to tick all the boxes on the 'gorgeous' list. A wonderfully uplifting piece of research by Albert Mehrabian and Jeffrey Blum at the University of California[6] discovered that, if you're looking for a partner, it's more important to take care of your appearance than it is to be conventionally good-looking. They showed 117 university students pictures of people and asked to rate them according to attractiveness. Surprisingly, by far the most attractive features were those considered 'self-care', such as good grooming, brushed hair, well-fitting clothes and good posture. In other words, stop torturing yourself by comparing yourself to Hollywood stars, all you need to do is run an iron over your clothes and stand up straight!

> *Stop torturing yourself by comparing yourself to Hollywood stars*

As well as this heartening evidence, one of the most fundamentally important things to remember is that you need to work on feeling good about yourself, regardless of whether you consider yourself to be a 1 or a 10 in terms of conventional beauty. It's human nature to search for flaws and imperfections in ourselves, but I would advise that you try to replace negative self-talk with more neutral observations. Swap: "My upper arms are flabby" or "My double chin is gross," with "My arms are strong," and "my face is appealing." Stop that drip-drip-drip of self-condemnation and start to think about the many wonderful attributes that you have that make you desirable. You'll soon find that your thoughts automatically become more positive about yourself and you then present a rosier picture to the world.

The Eye of the Beholder

Belle, from southeast Asia, never really felt beautiful as she was growing up, and this was probably because her parents didn't seem to be proud of her or compliment her in any way. So it's fair to say that her self-esteem was at rock bottom. At school, she felt like she was always a shadow behind the other, prettier girls, who were quick to seize on this insecurity and use it to keep her in her place. Yet in her own way, Belle was attractive – her skin had a natural glow and her hair was long and glossy. She just didn't know she was lovely, because nobody told her.

When she started dating as an adult, she realised that she wanted to find a man who had life experiences beyond the world she grew up in. She found her own culture suffocating, and the traditional roles of men and women very limiting. She wanted that elusive 'westerner' – a man who would show her a different life from the one she had been living. So when she met Joe, an Australian, from the first moment that he showed her any kindness, she fell for him. She didn't care that to other women, Joe was perhaps not the most attractive of men – to her he was wonderful. She felt lucky that he even paid attention to her, and because of this low self-regard, she put Joe on a pedestal. In her eyes, he was her Prince Charming.

As the years passed, their relationship bloomed. Belle didn't mind at all when middle-age spread set in and Joe started looking older and a little care-worn. For her, this only served to confirm in her mind that they would stay together forever, as it meant that

THE EXTERIOR OF YOUR HOUSE

Joe would not be attractive to other women – because, despite the fact that Joe regularly told Belle how beautiful she was, she never quite believed him. Nonetheless, Belle did gain in confidence over the years and did gain some self-belief. You could say she became the Cinderella to his Prince Charming, and they did live happily ever after (or at least, they're still going strong).

I'm sharing this story with you for two reasons. Firstly, Belle and Joe were attracted to each other because of their ordinariness not in spite of it. The fact that neither of them outshone the other provided firm foundations for their house of love. Joe found Belle beautiful, and she loved his cultural other-worldliness. This was enough to cement their relationship. Yet what I think it also shows is that even if you don't believe you are attractive, even if your parents and your friends have always derided you for some reason, you will be attractive to someone; you can find love, because beauty always has been and always will be in the eye of the beholder.

Learn to Speak Body Language

It's cheering to realise that however important appearance is in society, we're all beautiful to someone. But what can we do to give ourselves an extra boost when we meet someone we like? Recent research shows that much of what we express is actually non-verbal, ie: how we walk, use our hands, smile or frown, speaks volumes about who we are. So, it's a good idea to take a look at our body language.

Crossing your legs may be your favourite way to sit comfortably, but did you realise you're also sending out potent signals to everyone around you? In fact, everything you do, from the way you wiggle your eyebrows to the direction you point your toes, says something about you. Once you become aware of your body language, not only can you influence how others view you, but you can also gain an insight into yourself too.

Body language is primarily unconscious – our brains have mirror neurons that fire when we register an emotion in someone else – before we're even aware of it. The secret to using body language to your advantage is by bringing it from your unconscious to your conscious mind, in other words, letting your unconscious do the heavy lifting and then tuning in to it. This is what we mean when we say we have a 'gut feeling' or 'instinct' – on a deeper level we have already registered the emotional temperature of the situation. Hundreds of years ago, before humans developed language, this was the only way we communicated, but since we learnt how to speak, body language has been pushed out of our conscious minds, but still remains a powerful force.

We all know the classic body language signals that

show we're interested in someone: lingering eye contact, smiling and so on; it's common sense, but when we're feeling anxious or vulnerable it's nigh on impossible to put them into practice. In social situations, it can be tempting to send the exact opposite messages, such as pointedly ignoring someone or adopting a haughty 'look but don't touch' demeanour because we're too nervous to think about sending out positive body language signals. This is the ultimate in self-sabotage. In the first instance, it's totally confusing to ignore someone you're interested in, and in the second case, the pose looks amazing in Vogue, but in real life, it says you're frosty.

So body language is an important skill to master. Using our 'home' analogy, consider this. What would you find more appealing: a house where the front door has a 'Welcome' mat, the curtains are open and there's a smell of freshly-brewed coffee emanating from an open window; or a house where the door's slammed firmly shut, the curtains are drawn and there are cobwebs on the windows. Take a minute to envisage those two scenarios and how they might translate in terms of body language, and you'll see just how important it is.

Eye Contact

Interestingly we're the only animals to always show the whites of our eyes, and it seems that is what makes our eyes far more expressive than any other body language signal. Take full advantage of your eyes' potency by catching someone else's eye, holding their gaze for one second then looking away and down to the left. This is a very powerful piece of body language and takes the tried and tested eye-contact strategy up a level. According to Neuro-Linguistic

Programming (NLP), looking to the left indicates recalling images and memories whilst looking to the right indicates constructive or creative thinking. So looking slightly down and left suggests you and this time, team it with a subtle smile.

Smile!

A genuine smile starts in your eyes – so don't fake it by just curving your mouth upwards, because you won't fool anybody (least of all, yourself). Cultivate your smile by imagining you've just seen your best friend. Forget your traditional 'selfie' grin or O-shaped pout; develop an authentic, signature smile that is warm yet sexy; but be careful not to overbear your teeth, or you'll look like an angry chimp!

The impact of a smile is not just about attracting a mate, it's also psychologically beneficial to you too. It was Charles Darwin who first noticed the connection between facial expressions and the emotions behind them, saying: "The free expression by outward signs of an emotion, intensifies it.[7]" In other words, it's like a chain reaction: if you feel happy, you smile and this makes you feel happier. We're very simple creatures really – our brain registers that we are smiling and thinks: "Oh, I must be happy, let's have a boost of endorphins." It's what scientists call a positive feedback loop.

Turn that frown upside down!

It also works in the reverse. In a hilarious piece of research by The University of Wales[8], it was discovered that people who had had Botox to reduce wrinkles on their foreheads reported feeling happier and less anxious. "Elementary!" say the Sherlock Holmes' among us. "They must have felt happier because they no longer had ugly frown lines." Not so, say the researchers, because the Botox fans say that feelings about their attractiveness were not affected. (Which makes you wonder why they did it in the first place, but still...) No, it was simply not being able to frown that made them happier. So, by simply turning that frown upside down, you can affect how people see you, and put a spring in your step too.

Posture

Did you know that instinctively, we clamp our elbows tightly by our sides when we're nervous as an unconscious way of giving ourselves a reassuring squeeze? Isn't that amazing! And we will often clutch a drink in front of us to form a barrier, if someone is getting a bit too close, but this can also come across as being closed and unapproachable. If you don't want to keep someone at bay at a party, try to relax your elbows instead, and hold your drink to one side. Balance your weight evenly between your feet and place them a few inches apart. Whether standing or sitting, keep your legs uncrossed, because crossed legs suggest you feel under pressure. Breathe out and roll your shoulders back and down. Angle your body towards someone you're interested in, to send 'come hither' signals, but only at 45 degrees: directly is too confrontational.

If you've set your sights on someone who is already a friend, it can be hard to tell the difference between 'friendly' and 'romantic' body language. One easy way around this is if, when he leaves a room, she/he glances back at you one last time – this lingering look means they can't get enough of you.

Mirroring

If you've managed to pluck up the courage to start chatting to someone, well done, you! Something you can do to ensure that the conversation goes as well as it possibly can, is to mirror them. So if they take a sip of their drink, you take one too – this increases the feeling that you are in synch with each other and are compatible. Equally, mirroring can be done unconsciously, so if you realise that the person you are chatting to is copying your body language, you can tell they're attracted to you.

Touch and Space

If you want to ramp things up a notch, try the 'face platter'. This is when you prop your elbows on the table and rest your chin on one hand – this pose presents your face as if on a plate and encourages the other person to admire it. Another way to get things moving is to gently introduce some physical contact. A study about the effect of touch[9] reveals that even just a gentle brush against someone's arm can work wonders in terms of indicating interest or affection. In the experiment, when someone was asked a question, if they were being lightly touched on the arm at the same time, they were more likely to give a favourable response. So don't resist the urge to gently touch, pat or tap someone to emphasise the fact that you're feeling good in their company.

I do want to inject a note of caution here however, because this has to be done in a very subtle way, as respecting someone's personal space is paramount, and some people may find such expressive touch an invasion of their space

– so be very careful to gauge the warmth and openness of the situation you're in first. Also, touching – however insignificantly or gently – can be misconstrued as a 'come on', so be aware of the potential for this to backfire. That said, a tiny gesture can reap dividends. We're all aware of our personal space, particularly when someone unwelcome invades it, but the study of it, called 'proxemics', has identified four different zones: public, social, personal and intimate. They all depend on how well you know the person you are talking to, but if your potential partner moves from 'personal' (2-4ft apart) to 'intimate' (0-2ft apart) you can be sure that they feel comfortable with you.

Monitoring their body language as well as your own can be tricky, but it can give you vital clues as to whether there's any frisson between you. A surefire way to tell if you're floating someone's boat is when they flash you. No, not like that! In body language terms this means raising your eyebrows for a fraction of a second, usually teamed with a smile. This is a primal greeting that says: "I acknowledge you and am not threatening," so say body-language experts Allan and Barbara Pease.[10]

Why not try putting your new found body language skills into practice and watch as each social gathering becomes alive with possibilities.

Punching Above Your Weight

We know that 'like attracts like' but are you one of those contrary people who aspires to meet someone more attractive or with higher social standing than yourself – or, to use the vernacular, do you like to 'punch above your weight'? There are several different reasons why people want to have a relationship with someone who they consider to be 'a catch', and psychologically, the motives can enter murky waters here. Psychologist Dr Seth Meyers[11] says that couples where one person is far more attractive than the other stand out from the crowd because we are programmed to believe that we should pick people of the same level of attractiveness. To discover how the impact of going outside this socially accepted norm may affect you, he suggests trying a visualisation exercise:

Imagine yourself entering a party with a gorgeous partner on your arm, someone who makes everyone around you go slack-jawed with desire. As you walk towards the drinks table, you notice all eyes are upon you. Except that when you look closer, you realise they're not, they're on your partner. As you become an observer in this spectacle of a crowd ogling your beautiful partner, how are you feeling? Proud that despite your average looks you have managed to appeal to someone so gorgeous? Or perhaps it makes you think that people assume that your partner is a gold-digger, only with you because you shower them with trinkets and holidays? Maybe it makes you feel insecure that everyone is mentally undressing your date with their eyes? After all, if you managed to persuade him/her to go out with you, doesn't that mean that anyone else could too?

All of these explanations are based on shaky foundations – the first may ultimately lead you to come to the conclusion that you are inadequate, the second puts your partner in a bad light and the third raises the ugly spectre of jealousy and paranoia. What at first may be an appealing prospect may eventually bring tension, insecurity and self-doubt into the relationship. So think very carefully before you decide to punch above your weight.

Dr Meyers suggests that the best or even only

situation for being in a relationship with someone more attractive than yourself is if you have a healthy, robust ego – you feel good about yourself, secure in your own appearance and sure that you offer an all-round likable package that doesn't require amazing looks. Ironically, the person who would find it easiest to date someone who may be considered much more attractive than them is someone who doesn't place much value on physical appearance. The fact that their partner is beautiful is secondary to the other characteristics that attract them.

The Chemistry of Attraction

Steve could have been a model – being tall, slim, blond, blue-eyed and American to boot. However, he felt he was better employed in the corporate world as he had a calm, analytical outlook on life. He was aware that he was attractive but wasn't arrogant about it and if asked, he would have rated himself around eight out of ten in terms of his looks. During one of his business trips, he met petite, pan-Asian, bright-eyed Sofia. He couldn't take his eyes off her. The feeling was mutual and the air between them was thick with the chemistry of attraction. They both instantly knew they had fallen for each other at first sight. Sofia, despite feeling somewhat 'vertically challenged' when standing next to Steve, felt that her exotic looks coupled with her bubbly personality made her an eight or a nine on the good-looks scale.

Their relationship quickly developed, despite the long distances between their respective homes. Invariably, when this beautiful couple went out on dates they would turn heads. On occasion, Steve would be furtively approached by beautiful girls asking for his number, and once, a modeling agency tried to enlist him! Instead of feeling threatened by this, Sofia was very proud that he attracted so much attention. She felt secure that she could hold Steve's affection because she believed herself to be beautiful and confident, and so she was – and it has to be said, she has enjoyed a fair degree of adulation from strangers too. She felt pleased that she had managed to find such an attractive partner because it reflected well on her and reassured her that she was a catch.

THE EXTERIOR OF YOUR HOUSE

This case study embodies all the principles we have discussed so far in the book: believing in yourself, exuding confidence, making the most of your natural assets, not punching above your weight... These are the foundations of a great relationship. In Steve and Sofia's case, there was an instant, undeniable chemistry between them and all the outside attention they received confirmed that they had chosen well; that they were equally attractive.

What Is Attractive To You?

Now you know the science behind it, and have read three accounts of how attractiveness influences decision-making in your love life, you might like to try the exercises below, that will help to identify what you are looking for in a partner, in terms of their appearance. Take a step back from the constant search for love and spend a moment in contemplation. It will help you become more aware of the unconscious undercurrents that influence your life choices.

> *Putting pen to paper helps to cement your thoughts more firmly and give you clarity about what you really want*

You may be tempted to do this in your head rather than writing it down, but there is a lot of scientific evidence to support the fact that putting pen to paper helps to cement your thoughts more firmly and give you clarity about what you really want. This is central to my whole philosophy – if you are clear about what your dreams are, then you can make them happen.

Give yourself 20 minutes of uninterrupted peace in a quiet, calm room, so you can devote yourself completely to these exercises.

THE EXTERIOR OF YOUR HOUSE

1. First, develop a clear understanding of what your views are about appearance, how they were created and what in particular you find attractive. To do this, think about your parents' looks and what it was about their appearance that is most striking to you. If you feel negative towards one or both of your parents, perhaps you shy away from their 'type'? For example, if your domineering father had dark hair and piercing eyes, you may gravitate towards people with fair hair and a gentle demeanour. Your mother and father are key figures in the development of your personality and identity, so examining what impact they've had on your feelings about appearance, both your own and other people's, will provides insights into what will make you happy in a relationship. Jot down a few lines about this.

_____
_____
_____
_____
_____
_____
_____
_____
_____
_____
_____
_____
_____
_____
_____
_____
_____

2. Turn your thoughts towards yourself and your own appearance. Do you unconsciously emulate one of your parents in style and taste? This suggests that you admire and respect their opinion and would like to be like them. Or, have you developed your own sense of style? This indicates that you have naturally moved away from needing your parents' approval. What has influenced your decisions about the way you look? Think carefully about this, as the answer will reveal what signals you are sending out to the world and also what you find attractive.

_____
_____
_____
_____
_____
_____
_____
_____
_____
_____
_____
_____
_____
_____
_____
_____
_____
_____
_____
_____
_____

THE EXTERIOR OF YOUR HOUSE

3. Then think about the society you grew up in and how different people's looks made you feel. Did you try to emulate the looks of a school friend, a pop star or a football hero? Add a few more lines. If you live in a conventional, even conservative environment, where there is pressure to conform that extends to dictating the way you dress, how does this make you feel? Claustrophobic or comfortable? If this doesn't apply to you, do you feel happy looking different to other people or do you feel safer as one of the flock?

_____
_____
_____
_____
_____
_____
_____
_____
_____
_____
_____
_____
_____
_____
_____
_____
_____
_____
_____
_____
_____

4. Now look over your answers and try to build a general overview of your feelings about appearance, how it has been influenced, and how it has evolved into what you look like right now. Are you happy with the way you look? If not, what can you do to change your appearance and attractiveness? It might be helpful to use the house analogy and think of this in terms of painting and decorating. You don't have to change fundamentally, but for everyone, there's always room for improvement. Write down your thoughts and reflections here.

_____
_____
_____
_____
_____
_____
_____
_____
_____
_____
_____
_____
_____
_____
_____
_____
_____
_____
_____
_____
_____
_____

THE EXTERIOR OF YOUR HOUSE

5. By undertaking this exercise, hopefully, you will discover assumptions and preferences that you had not been previously aware of and this will help guide you in your active search for your ideal partner. The next step is to investigate your relationship history to search for clues that will reveal your secret desires.

Looking back at your last three partners (if possible), what attracted you to them physically? What was the first impression they made on you? Is there a similar theme that connects them all or are they all different?

_____
_____
_____
_____
_____
_____
_____
_____
_____
_____
_____
_____
_____
_____
_____
_____
_____
_____
_____
_____

6. Finally, what physical attributes are you most attracted to? Choose your top three. Now, if you could create the looks of a perfect partner, what would he/she look like? Be creative: will they be dark or fair, slim or muscular? Are they left-handed? What is their skin tone? From the tip of his/her head to their toes, try to visualise exactly what they look like.

Before I met my partner, I tried this exercise and imagined a blond-haired, blue-eyed Swedish man called Sven. To keep my options open, and for a bit of fun, I also threw into the pot another ideal man, totally different from the first in that I imagined a dark-haired drum-playing, samba dancer! The universe obviously listened to both my requests as some time afterwards, I met my future husband, who is a mix of my two perfect men – a dark-haired, blue-eyed Scandinavian drummer! I'm adding this reflection on my own life to reassure you that there is a good reason for doing this exercise, because I have found that often, as you ask, so shall you receive. That's why it's important to be careful what you wish for!

See It, Believe It, Achieve It!

By now, you will have a fully rounded image of the type of person you would like to meet. So now what? What are you supposed to do with this information apart from dream of your wedding day? Social and behavioural scientist Frank Niles[12] says that the reason why this visualisation exercise is so helpful is because you are creating a mental image of a 'goal' – and that goal is your ideal partner. When you can see your goal, you begin to believe in the possibility of achieving it. This gives you the motivation and energy to pursue your goal actively rather than just yearning for it.

To explain the science behind visualisation, it works because when we imagine an act, our brain generates an impulse that tells our neurons (cells that transmit information) to perform the given scenario. This creates a new neural pathway in our brain that tells us that we have already achieved that goal. For example, the golfer Tiger Woods is a big fan of visualisation, and before he takes a shot, he visualises exactly where he would like the ball to land. This imagery enables his brain to instruct his body to complete the shot successfully, because it is already familiar with the end goal.

In other words, visualisation isn't just about feeling optimistic, it's about how preparation and rehearsal is genuinely a step closer towards achieving your dreams.

CHAPTER TWO

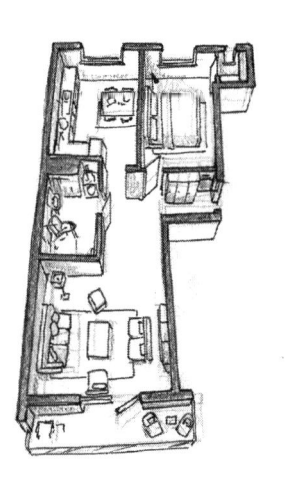

THE LAYOUT OF YOUR HOUSE

Being Truly At Home

There's nothing more revealing about a person's home than the moment you walk over their threshold, because it's an instant snapshot of all that the house contains. In that one moment, you will be able to gauge the emotional temperature within the house, the spaciousness (or not) of the layout, and the artistic temperament of the inhabitants. Even the smell of it gives us valuable clues about the people living therein – do you get a waft of something delicious cooking or is it more 'eau de damp'? Is it open-plan, airy and uncluttered or is it small, dark and cosy?

In the same way, when you get to know someone's emotional makeup you gain a glimpse of who they really are, on a fundamental level. I think that applying the analogy of the layout of a house really helps you to understand both your own emotional type and also that of the person you are ideally suited to. Visualising the type of home you would feel comfortable in gives you an insight into who you really are. In my coaching work, I often find that my clients have never really thought about what it is that makes them tick. I find it fascinating that we can be actively looking for someone who we want to get to know better, without even getting to know ourselves first!

The house visualisation tool that I have devised bypasses all the usual clichés about what makes someone attractive (gorgeous, rich, successful, and so on) and allows you to get right to the heart of the matter – are you compatible? Does this person make you feel truly 'at home'? After all, what is the point of moving into a penthouse apartment with wall-to-wall glass and shiny surfaces just because it looks impressive when what the real you – your soul or your essence – craves is the comfort and security of a thatched cottage? Remember Vicky and Ian's story in Chapter One? Neither was drop-dead gorgeous but they found each other and have built a loving relationship based on a shared love of fitness. I'd imagine that the home they share is likely to have a mini-gym in the garage, at the very least.

> *Does this person make you feel truly 'at home'?*

Throughout this book, I want to emphasise a fundamental point there is no 'wrong' answer and equally no 'wrong' type of person – everyone has something to offer and you do not have to change to find happiness. All I hope to do is to give you a nudge in the right direction, helping you to open your eyes to who you are and what you want.

This chapter will enable you to get to grips with the wide range of emotional types there are, out there in the big wide world: from someone who flings the front door open and starts chatting ten to the dozen, sharing their whole life story with you (that's me, folks!), to the person who peeps through the letterbox before cautiously opening the door, whilst avoiding eye contact.

As well as helping you become more perceptive and intuitive about other people, becoming emotionally aware about yourself is like unlocking the door to future happiness, especially when it comes to love. Taking an honest, unflinching look at what has influenced you to make you the (wonderful) person you are will be a window into your psyche, enabling you to realise who and what can make you feel complete.

> *Becoming emotionally aware is like unlocking the door to future happiness*

So now I invite you to become your own therapist, asking all the incisive questions that reveal the true you. Sometimes the answers will surprise you and sometimes you'll already be familiar with them, but focused consideration of all aspects of your emotional makeup can help to unravel the patterns in your life and once you're aware of these patterns, you can evaluate who would make a good match for you. So what's the first question any therapist asks?

Tell Me About Your Family

We all know what Philip Larkin thinks about mums and dads (or if you don't, please read his famous poem This *Be the Verse* for a brilliantly caustic view of parenthood), but what can you remember about your childhood, specifically your family home? This may feel a bit random – are you wondering how this is relevant to finding love? Trust me, it's not only a brilliant way of summing-up a complicated and multifaceted experience, but by looking at the past, you can also learn valuable lessons to help create a positive future. So try to picture the house where you grew up. Was it light and airy? Did you feel like you could run around freely? Were your drawings pinned up on the kitchen wall? Was there a little corner that you could chill out in, that your dad had made all cosy, just for you? Or maybe it was rather dark and forbidding? Perhaps it was always cold, because your parents never put the heating on? Did the rooms and hallways feel maze-like and tough to navigate? Were children banned from certain rooms?

Thinking about how your childhood home made you feel can serve as a mirror, reflecting how you were affected emotionally by your parents who were, after all, the first major influences in your life. It also tells you how confident and secure you felt as a child, and how this has influenced your decision-making right now. Smashing Pumpkins frontman Billy Corgan said about his childhood: "I grew up in a house of no love or emotion – it kind of sticks with you." That is such a revealing comment and I admire his honesty in sharing this with us. Billy is the band's main songwriter and his lyrics have been called 'cathartic', so it seems he uses writing and music to express and come to terms with his childhood trauma.

Conversely, I have a friend who told me of her childhood in a small village in Oxfordshire in the 1970s, where the front door was always open to visitors, where in the summer, the children and their friends spent night after night sleeping in the back garden under the stars, and that they were allowed to cycle to the next village to visit friends, without adult supervision. My friend feels very strongly that her childhood gave her self-confidence, an ability to mix easily with people and perhaps most tellingly, she still prefers being outdoors to indoors, to this day.

So, I ask you to now reflect on your own childhood. Why not write down some thoughts and feelings about your home, your bedroom, your family and the significant or ordinary events that have helped to shape the person you are today. I hope you enjoy this trip down memory lane, as it may be quite revealing.

Now, let's focus on your adult life. Think about the room layout of the homes of your previous partners. Did any of them mirror your childhood home? Perhaps you were subconsciously looking for the comfort of a familiar environment – or maybe you felt attracted to this person because you recognised something within them? At the time it may have felt like a coincidence, but we don't need to be Sigmund Freud to realise that we all unconsciously gravitate to people who remind us of our parents. Whether this ultimately affects the relationship positively or negatively is secondary to the fact that we are drawn towards the familiar. (Which reminds me of that great joke: what is the definition of a Freudian slip? To say one word when you mean to say a mother!)

> *We're not aware that we are repeating the patterns learnt in our childhood*

A study by psychologist Glenn Geher[13] tested Freud's theory by not only asking people to identify traits shared by both their partners and their parents, but also interviewing the parents themselves. He discovered that there was robust evidence to suggest that romantic partners have lots of the same characteristics as one or both parents. Geher also went on to conclude that if the characteristics were positive, then the romantic relationship was more likely to be harmonious; but if the traits were negative then there was trouble ahead. It makes sense that if your dad was physically strong and able to fix anything that went wrong then you might expect your partner to be similarly talented, or that if your mother was glamorous and always had beautiful hair, that would be the norm for any partner. Conversely, if your mother was a raging alcoholic, then you're likely to be uncomfortable around drink, or if your father lost his temper at the drop of a hat, that you might be anxious about not irritating your partner – although quite why you'd choose a partner with such negative traits is a whole other book altogether…

Ironically, since choosing our partners because they remind us of our parents isn't a conscious decision, we're not aware that we are repeating the patterns learnt in our

THE LAYOUT OF YOUR HOUSE

childhood. Sometimes it's only when we sit down and look at how our relationships have turned out that we realise that our parents' emotional types (as well as their politics and their opinions) have had such a profound impact on us. Read Brian's poignant story below to discover how we can only have 20/20 vision in hindsight.

When Your Head Rules Your Heart

Brian's parents were two highly intelligent and competent professionals, who competed with each other in the same academic field. They were very career-driven and Brian hardly saw much of them when he was growing up. On the rare occasions that they all sat down together for a meal, Brian would never be asked how his day was or what he would like to do at the weekend – instead the conversation revolved around politics and academia. If Brian wanted to engage with his parents, he had no choice but to join the debate on their level, where the topics were discussed within very rigid parameters and the tone was always argumentative and strident.

With very little emotional input from his parents, it was perhaps inevitable that Brian should adopt the same communication style as them, and that their beliefs shaped his own views. It was unfortunate that their priorities were skewed and emphasis was placed on knowledge and truth being paramount, rather than love.

As an adult, Brian repeated this way of interacting in each of his relationships. He was more concerned about arguing the point and its merits than really listening to his partner's feelings. However, it was a huge shock for Brian when his parents' marriage failed after 35 years together. It made him re-evaluate his admiration for them. Realising that he related to them as professional academics, and not as loving parents was a painful understanding, and he became aware that his own failed relationships reflected that of his parents.

THE LAYOUT OF YOUR HOUSE

Only now, as a single father, has he realised that it's not important to be right if it's at the expense of another person's feelings. Instead, the focus should be on making the other party feel that they are being listened to and that it is who they are that is important. With this new sensitivity, Brian is optimistic for the future and hopes to finally find the right partner who will help him develop his emotional awareness as well as sharing his ideas and intellect.

What's Your Emotional Type?

Brian's rocky relationship history was largely due to not being encouraged to share his feelings as a child. As a consequence, he developed a very restricted emotional repertoire and was a difficult person to have a relationship with. Hopefully, now he has become aware of this, things will improve, but it goes to show how important having some insight into how you engage with the world really is.

Learning to recognise what sort of temperament you have (and what you are attracted to) is an important skill because it can help explain why you click with some people while others completely grate on you. Consider a super-confident career woman making a beeline for a cautious librarian – you know sparks are unlikely to fly.

This is why I've devised a series of archetypes to guide you, based on my life experiences. I consider myself to be a global nomad, having lived all around the world, including Singapore, Malaysia, China, The Netherlands, Germany, France, Switzerland and England, and during my adventures I've learned much more about emotional intelligence, and how it varies from country to country. This has led me to develop a theory that the different cultural archetypes of the world actually reflect the places they live in. This is partly why I wrote this book using the 'architect' analogy and also because it's such an interesting concept: a bit like the chicken and the egg – did people develop their dwellings to suit their emotional styles or was it vice versa?

Obviously, I know that there are many, many people who don't fit into the archetype of their country of origin, and I truly do not wish to offend anyone, so see this as a 'tool for understanding' just as some people use astrology to understand different archetypes. This tool will help you identify which emotional type you are, but don't feel restricted by your nationality – it's perfectly possible to be Asian yet have a Scandinavian outlook on life! Equally, you can pick and mix from different categories. The main idea is to discover which category you gravitate towards to help you gain an insight into your temperament. Since it's my heritage we'll start with the tropics.

The tropical emotional type

People who live in countries around the tropics are hot-blooded, passionate and wear their hearts on their sleeve; they tend not to have hidden depths, preferring to keep feelings out in the open. This chimes with their environment perfectly because living in the tropics means being used to intense heat and humidity, so clothing is kept to a minimum and people are never swaddled or covered up in layers of material. There is a natural sensuality to people who live in the warmer climes: they are open about their bodies, because they're rarely covered up. To help cope with the heat, dwellings are often open-plan, to let the little air that there is circulate. Living spaces and bedrooms are communal and there is very little privacy – often, everyone lives on top of each other, which results in lots of raised voices and hot-tempers, which quickly subside. Parents are quite likely to raise their voices at their kids but then they'll also give them a big hug and tell them they love them too. When a group of women from my home country, Singapore, get together, they all talk nonstop, often interrupting or talking over each other, revealing all sorts of intimate details about sex and relationships that would make your eyes water – something that's not that common in our cooler-region friends.

Key words: open, extrovert, expressive, sensual, hot-tempered

The Scandinavian/North European Emotional Type

The typical characteristics of people from these cooler regions are directness, plain-speaking but with emotional reserve. The weather can be very chilly and so the houses are very well insulated and heated, suggesting the type of personality that is warm underneath several layers of practicality. In Seattle, USA, where there is a large Nordic-heritage population, there is what is known as 'The Seattle Freeze', describing the frosty reception visitors to that town might receive and their jokey slogan is: 'Have a nice day. Somewhere else.'[14]

The living areas of Scandinavian homes are often highly functional, uncluttered and open-plan and there are bedrooms that allow for everyone's own private space. I remember taking an evening stroll in a small town in Holland where I was living at the time, and wondering why everyone had their curtains open, enabling me to see everything that was going on inside. A Dutch friend explained that this habit derives from their Calvinist sensibility – a branch of Christianity that encourages a somewhat austere, disciplined lifestyle. People with a Calvinist upbringing are happy to reveal their homes to the world as proof that they are law-abiding, clean-living citizens, not getting up to any mischief behind those curtains.

Key words: measured, no-nonsense, reserved, hidden-depths, mysterious

The English emotional type

Take a look at the rows and rows of Victorian houses in much of England, all squashed up together, and you get an idea of the personality of the inhabitant. Inside, the house is divided into lots of different rooms, each with their own purpose – dining room, sitting room, kitchen – giving a sense of orderliness. The rooms themselves are often adorned with furniture, curtains, cushions and knick-knacks. 'An Englishman's home is his castle', and whilst this may be seen as a barricade from the outside world – the need for privacy – it is also where people express themselves creatively. England is world-renowned for the beauty of its gardens, for example.

Whilst the 'castle' analogy indicates a need for privacy and the tendency to draw-up the emotional drawbridge at times, it also shows a strong desire to protect and nurture the family within. The traditional stiff upper lip that helped them through two world wars shows a tendency for bravery and stoicism in the face of adversity but it also means the Brits do not readily reveal emotions, generally. There is a stereotype that English people are overly concerned with public appearances and thus are polite and apologetic – preferring never to cause 'a scene' – a British queue being world famous – yet, the underdog in any scenario will be fiercely championed by them, suggesting a deep regard for justice and fairness in all things.

Key words: private, polite, creative, protective, fair

The American emotional type

'The American Dream' exemplifies this nation's ethos – that is, anything can be achieved through hard work, regardless of who you are and what your background is. This optimistic outlook means that you can build your own (often detached) house or for city-dwellers, renovate your own loft apartment and this relates to a central belief in being self-reliant.

The property's gleaming appearance, with all the mod-cons you could possibly desire, reveals a need to proudly display all the evidence of your hard work and abilities, which can sometimes be interpreted as boastfulness and arrogance. Because of this emphasis on success and conspicuous wealth, American people are understandably focused and driven with high expectations of themselves and others. The classic white-picket fence depicted in so many American films suggests that they are independent and protective of their family and possessions. They do not hesitate to hold back when something displeases them and are comfortable articulating what they need to be happy.

Key words: Proud, driven, independent, optimistic, self-assured

Obviously, I haven't covered every country or region here, but I hope from this brief overview that you get the drift of my theory: that our environment – both natural and built – influences us in myriad ways. As W. Clement Stone said, "You are a product of your environment," but he also went on to say that we can choose the environment that best suits our objectives, and that we must analyse what is holding us back, and what we want to change. I find this really motivational.

Now you've studied these cultural archetypes, it is a good idea to begin to draw a picture of your own emotional type and also that of your potential soulmate, because it really helps to keep this awareness in the forefront of your mind. Check out the exercises at the end of the chapter to help build a bigger picture of what makes you, *You*

WHEN LOVE BREAKS DOWN

It's a sad fact of life that sometimes relationships break down. This can be due to many factors, but often differing emotional types is a major reason. One person's love of solitude and peace may be interpreted as another person's rejection and unavailability. Happily, differing emotional types may still be compatible if each partner is aware of the other's needs and has the sensitivity to go outside their own comfort zone to provide them. Take Brian's story, above. If he meets a new partner who understands his deeply rooted habit of intellectualising everything, then he/she may be accommodating of this, so long as Brian also makes an effort to listen to his partner's needs and respects their own emotional type.

> *One person's love of solitude and peace may be interpreted as another person's rejection and unavailability*

Ground breaking psychologist Edward de Bono said: "Studies have shown that 90% of error in thinking is due to error in perception. If you can change your perception, you can change your emotion and this can lead to new ideas."[15]

This is so true, especially with regard to relationships: if you try to see your view of the world as one that isn't set in stone, but is influenced by many different factors and open to readjustment, then you will be much more empathetic towards other people, and empathy is absolutely key in good relationships.

So, it is vitally important to develop ways of communicating that allow each person to express what they need in the relationship. Read Teya's story below to discover how a marriage can go awry so easily without continual maintenance and understanding of both party's emotional checklist.

A Marriage of Two Halves

When Dean started showing an interest in Teya, she didn't really take much notice, she was too busy concentrating on earning enough money to support herself and her elderly parents. She found it hard to believe that Dean, who she knew was financially successful and owned several businesses, would seriously be interested in her. However, he kept pursuing her, convinced that they would be together. He was so confident in this that he even talked about starting a family on their first date.

Dean viewed courtship in the same way he approached business – with a single-minded determination to succeed. His persistence paid off and Teya agreed to date him and then, to marry him. Sadly, as time went by, she became aware that Dean did not make her happy, because he seemed indifferent to her needs. She had tried her best to love him but realised that his initial enthusiasm towards her was due to the fact that he was looking for a woman to bear him children, rather than a wife to cherish. Added to this, their different cultural backgrounds meant that their emotional types were incompatible. Dean being a typically private English man, found it hard to express his feelings either in words or by being physically affectionate, whilst Teya being an expressive Thai-heritaged woman found his inability to express his emotions very frustrating, wishing he could just hug her more often than she hugged her pillow to sleep at night.

If the truth be told, Teya felt alone in the

marriage. After more than 20 years together, she wanted out. Yet due to the years of never really being emotionally honest with each other, she is still trying to pluck up the courage to discuss this with Dean, who undoubtedly has drawn-up his emotional drawbridge. If Teya does find the strength to face Dean and be honest about her emotional needs, will Dean be able to re-evaluate his perception of their relationship and respond to Teya accordingly? And similarly, will Teya be able to transcend her cultural deference to men, and in future, be honest with Dean about her needs?

Making Your Emotions Work For You

Learning how to build connections between yourself and a potential soulmate is a fundamental building block of a relationship. After the initial electrical charge of attraction has passed, it's time to start forging a deep emotional synergy, where both you and your partner feel understood, respected and loved.

One of the most important ways of developing this is with emotional intelligence. A popular buzzword in psychological circles, also known as your EQ, this term first made an appearance in the 1960s but gained popularity 30 years later when psychologist Daniel Goleman wrote a book of the same name[16]. EQ is defined as the ability to identify and manage your own emotions, to be aware of others' emotions and use this information to guide your behaviour. This last part is the crucial one, I think. It's all very well being aware of your feelings, but actually translating this thought into action in a social setting is the real test. It's easy to say: "I find the way my partner's job interferes with our home life very annoying," – the key is to look at why you are annoyed, analyse what tactics you can put in place to lessen the feelings of frustration and ultimately, discuss with your partner what can be done to alleviate your concerns whilst still allowing her to fulfil her obligations. This is a rational and practical response to feelings of annoyance and frustration and shows competent levels of EQ.

Let's compare a 'normal' exchange to an emotionally intelligent one in a situation where one partner finds their mother-in-law unbearably irritating.

Normal interaction:
Partner's mother: Haven't you had enough cake? Your trousers already look a bit tight.
Your emotional response: A feeling of being attacked about your weight, resulting in defensiveness and anger.
Your reaction: Either expressed as a snide comeback, eg: "Hark at the kettle calling the pot black," or by retreating into a sulking ball of resentment, further compounding your dislike of her.

Emotionally intelligent interaction:
Partner's mother: Haven't you had enough cake? Your trousers already look a bit tight.
Your emotional response: A feeling of being attacked, followed by the reflection that your mother-in-law is awkward in social situations, often says the wrong thing, and is from a different generation who thinks it's acceptable to comment on physical appearance. In your heart you know she wants the best for you, and that she is showing her love for you, albeit in a roundabout way.
Your reaction: Deflect and gently steer away from this topic with humour: "I bet you're only saying that because you want the last slice." (A joke can often help diffuse tension.) Then deftly change the subject: "Anyway, how are your runner beans doing? Lots of slugs this year, I'm told." This response acknowledges her comment and protects yourself from further attack whilst continuing the conversation and encouraging your partner's mother to participate on a safer subject.

Taking a step back and reining-in your usual emotional response can be a huge challenge, particularly during strained occasions, but with practise, it can be done. It's not about suppressing your emotions – and they'll always find a way to bubble up anyway – but it is a matter of learning to read your emotions and understand where they have come from. Sometimes the sudden surge of anger, sadness or anxiety hasn't even been provoked by the person you're talking to, but instead triggered by a memory, eg: 'My mum always rationed cake and biscuits, and it felt so unfair as a child – now someone else is trying to do this and I'm an adult. I don't want to have these painful feelings again.' So you lash out or feel wounded much more dramatically than you would if this didn't touch an emotional nerve.

So try to get into the habit of taking a second to examine where the emotion has come from – in both parties, not just yourself. At first it can seem difficult but with practise you'll start doing it automatically and give yourself an extra boost both emotionally and socially. Not only that, but the more often you can do this, the better all your relationships will become, and what is miraculous – remember, 'What comes round really does go round' – is that your good example will rub-off on your partner too, who will in turn become more emotionally intelligent in their own responses.

Another great thing about emotional intelligence is that you can actively apply it to increase your attractiveness to other people. This may seem like an artificial and therefore false thing to do, akin to those cheesy tips about firm handshakes, but in reality all you're doing is tweaking how you behave on a very general level. I remember reading an article about how to get a boyfriend in a teen mag years ago, and the advice was to develop a sudden interest in football/cricket/basketball so you can impress him with your newfound knowledge of his favourite hobby! This strikes me as totally unnecessary and tedious, especially if the interest is completely feigned. It also has the rather grim underlying message that what you already have to offer is not good enough. However, the emotionally intelligent solution to this would be to simply ask him questions about his hobby – then he feels acknowledged, opens up to you and you create a connection – you don't need to be knowledgeable about it for him to feel appreciated. When you're a couple and you're sick to death of going to football matches, then it's time for another chat about compromise in the relationship, but that's another matter…

> *Emotional intelligence can be actively applied to increase your attractiveness*

Here's a quick run-down on the main principles of applying emotional intelligence in social situations.

Really Listen

According to an excellent article by Travis Bradberry on the Forbes website[17], listening and asking questions is the primary tool of the likeable person. So often it can feel like the other person is not engaging with what you're saying; that they are just biding time, waiting for a gap in the conversation so they can share their two-pennies' worth. To make someone feel 'heard', focus on what they are saying, reflect on it and ask them for more details. Try to avoid an interrogative style, aim for the gently probing approach and you're on to a winner.

Ignore technology

It may be beeping, ringing or vibrating, but resist the temptation to check your phone when you're talking to someone – anyone! A fascinating study in the US[18] revealed that while 89% of participants admitted to using their phones during a social gathering, 82% of that figure were aware that doing so had a negative impact on the conversation. We all know the feeling – it's insulting that the phone takes priority over real-life interaction, especially if they're only looking at pictures of cats in hats, or other inane stuff. And what about the side-splitting anecdote you're in the middle of telling? As soon as there's a ping on the phone, you've lost your audience, or worse still, they pretend to still be engaged in the story, whilst furtively replying 'lol' to another comedian, via text.

Respect the other person by putting away your phone and being *fully present* with them.

Be sincere

Whilst everyone has slightly different modes of being depending on where they are (we all have a veritable cloakroom of different hats we wear: an efficient employee hat, an entertaining friend hat, a supportive relative hat…), at the core of this must be an honest and genuine foundation of the real you. People warm to those who express themselves with sincerity because they feel trustworthy. Don't attempt to predict what will make someone like you, instead have the courage to show the world both your strengths and your vulnerabilities and people will genuinely want to get to know you.

Make a connection

In his fabulous book, *59 Seconds: Think a Little, Change a Lot*[19], Richard Wiseman identified keys reasons why people are more likely to be successful at interview. Surprisingly, being experienced or have squillions of qualifications wasn't as important as the ability to make a connection with the interviewer. Equally, that stands in other relationships. Finding common ground and enjoying discussing it is like discovering a life raft when you're lost at sea – such a relief! My husband and I have a shared love of watching comedies, whether its films, sit-coms or live stand-up. We really reconnect through the shared experience of laughter (which is, after all, the best medicine), and afterwards feel a warmth for each other, which can sometimes get lost in the busy-ness of every day. This is no mere 'wives-tale' either: laughing actually makes your brain release endorphins[20], our very own feel-good drug, so it's a win-win situation.

> *Finding common ground and enjoying discussing it is like discovering a life raft when you're lost at sea*

Have an open mind

Everyone is brought up with inherited judgments about the world. Ask yourself what yours are. Do you have a knee-jerk reaction about people of a different class to you? Are you envious or critical about other types of lifestyle? There are a million ways to judge other people, from the weighty issues – what their politics are – to the trivial, such as what sort of shoes they're wearing. Try to take off your 'judgey pants' and be open-minded about other people's choices. They may not be to your taste but they have a right to express them as much as you do. Being receptive to others will make you more approachable and interesting and you may just find that you meet someone perfect for you who you would previously have dismissed.

Liz and Rick's story, below, is a heartening example of how remaining optimistic about the potential for love always reaps dividends, despite many obstacles that life throws in the way.

Honesty is the Best Policy

Liz shared a story with me from the very early days of her relationship with Rick. Despite being married for over 25 years now, their relationship started off with a rocky patch. In fact, two rocky patches. The first time was when they were at university together and Rick failed to mention that he was having a long-distance relationship with someone else when he started going out with Liz. She broke it off as she felt that he needed to be honest with this girl and with himself. Liz was much more emotionally intelligent than Rick and understood what drove his behaviour more clearly than Rick did himself.

A couple of years later they got together again, because Liz just somehow knew that Rick was the one for her despite certain differences. Rick wanted to show Liz that he was serious about their relationship this time, and so he offered to move in with her. She agreed but once again felt doubtful as to how genuine he was when he literally brought only a small bag of clothes to her home – one pair of trousers was all he had! Liz knew that that one pair of trousers meant he wasn't emotionally ready to commit to her so she found an opportunity to raise the subject with him. Rick found it hard to admit that he only brought one pair of trousers with him because he was afraid that after what happened the last time they were together, she wouldn't trust him, and that ultimately, he would lose her again. Liz understood then that Rick had learned his lesson about commitment and just needed her reassurance that she had forgiven him.

THE LAYOUT OF YOUR HOUSE

Six weeks later, Rick got a job offer in the Middle East. This time round, Liz actively made a decision that would preserve the budding relationship. She agreed to move with him to give them the best chance of making the relationship work. Even though their emotional types were different, they had shared their feelings in an emotionally intelligent way, so Liz felt much more secure in the relationship. She told me that they were both keen to work through any differences by communicating their feelings and focusing on their common goals. They are now happily living in the tropics, despite their shaky start and I think this goes to prove that a little bit of emotional intelligence goes a long way.

How Do You Process Your Emotions?

We've had a good look at the fascinating emotional world inside us all and you've had a chance to examine what makes people click, so with all this information fresh in your mind, it's a good opportunity to take a few moments to contemplate what makes you tick, emotionally. As with the previous exercises, make sure you set aside some time alone, in a quiet place to let yourself focus on these points below – you'll reap the benefits if you do. 10 to 20 minutes is the optimum time to be able to concentrate on a single task – any longer and your attention starts to drift – so these 20 minutes really will be time well spent. It's no accident that those world-famous TED talks are limited to a maximum of 18 minutes!

THE LAYOUT OF YOUR HOUSE

1. If you haven't already done this earlier in the chapter, take some time now to envisage your ideal home. What does it look like inside? Describe it, detailing where it is similar to your childhood home, and where it differs. Now think about how these attributes relate to your ideal partner (warm, sunny, modern, or shabby chic...) Be playful and imaginative: does a pristine modern kitchen relate to a clean-shaven businessman in your eyes or does an exotic boudoir complete with Moroccan lamps and rugs relate to someone who loves travelling? I don't want you to rule-out any potential partner who doesn't live up to these expectations, but it just helps you to be aware of what you find attractive, and what you don't.

THE ARCHITECT OF LOVE

2. Think about your favourite song. If possible, play it so that all its differentelements come alive again – the chorus, the melody, the rhythm. Now listen to the lyrics – is there a message to the song that you particularly relate to? Songs have particularly strong emotional triggers – a Finnish study[21] discovered that when people listen to music, not only are the auditory areas of their brains activated, but also the areas connected with emotion, memory and creativity, so you're not just listening to the song, but you're also experiencing the feelings it conjures too. What is it about this particular song that resonates with you? How does it make you feel? Now imagine your potential partner has his/her own favourite song. Are you willing to 'dance' to a different tune? What is your reaction if your partner tunes-in to something you wouldn't usually listen to? How willing are you to be flexible and open your heart and mind to other influences? Taking this musical metaphor a step further, are there any musical genres or character traits in a person that you definitely couldn't relate to?

_____
_____
_____
_____
_____
_____
_____
_____
_____
_____
_____
_____

THE LAYOUT OF YOUR HOUSE

3. No matter what your country of origin is, what emotional type do you feel most accurately reflects you? Are you a typical English rose, or a Nordic mystery? What emotional type most attracts you, and why? Are you attracted to someone from a similar cultural background, or are you one of life's explorers, attracted to and curious about different cultures? Take some time to reflect on your emotional type as it will allow you to understand more deeply what makes you tick, and what you find attractive in others.

___
___
___
___
___
___
___
___
___
___
___
___
___
___
___
___
___
___
___
___
___
___
___

THE ARCHITECT OF LOVE

4. Finally, can you remember a time where you really listened to somebody; where you stopped talking and really heard what they were saying to you? Who was this person? Was she your friend, your nephew, your mother? What did it feel like to step back, shut up and listen? In what situation might you be able to repeat that level of emotional intelligence? If you met a potential partner, what traits would you look for in them to give you an indication of their emotional intelligence, and how would you indicate to them that you too are looking for a depth of self-awareness in your relationships?

CHAPTER THREE

HOW YOU FURNISH YOUR HOUSE

A Meeting of Minds

So now you have your dream house, but what's inside it? The 'hard furnishings' you have around you are also an important element of your home, and this is because they serve a crucial purpose. If you're an avid reader, then there will be plenty of bookcases. You're a film buff? Then you'll need a squashy sofa and wide-screen TV. In the same way, your intellect also provides a vital function in that it enables you to engage with the world.

In the 'house' analogy that's running through this book, I see hard furnishings – furniture, fitted kitchens and appliances – as equivalent to the reasoning and logical element of ourselves. We don't often change our furniture and in the same way, our intellects are stable too. There is room to manoeuvre, of course; we may choose to upgrade to a new leather corner-sofa in the same way that we may decide to take an evening class, but generally, once we've plumped for our dining table or our fitted kitchen, they're here to stay for a good few years.

How our intellect affects our relationships is an intriguing question, and one that I struggled with for a while. Our intellect is quite different to our emotions – those fluid, unpredictable things that often bubble up from sub-conscious sources – instead, intellect is grounded firmly in our rational side and is much less likely to be affected by events around us. To touch on the previous chapter, to gauge the emotional temperature of someone, you can use many different tools, such as studying body language and tone of voice, but a person's intellect only becomes apparent through talking to them and getting to know them. Examining your intellect is a key part of moving towards finding the ultimate, fulfilling relationship, because *our intellect controls how we communicate*.

Our reasoning ability is a huge factor in how smoothly our interactions are with friends, family, colleagues and lovers. Being diplomatic and having the ability to negotiate relies heavily on our intellect; without it, we would dissolve into an impulsive, chaotic, contrary mess. Similarly, making the most of our intellect allows us to blossom as a person, which is attractive to potential partners, but more of that later.

> *Our intellect controls how we communicate*

For those of you who are starting to feel anxious about your intellectual abilities because you didn't do particularly well at school or find it hard to follow what they say on *Newsnight*, I want to reassure you. It is NOT about how many academic qualifications you have or whether you can do the cryptic crossword, it is more about being able to apply logic to a situation to find a solution. Equally, I am not concerned about whether you are interested in classical music or pop, Shakespeare or *Fifty Shades of Grey*, because I'm not talking here about cultural preferences – I'm talking about the ability to think clearly about yourself, your life and your aspirations.

To be sure, there is a certain amount of snobbery out there about what makes you an intellectual, but whether your interests are considered high-brow or low-brow, enjoying something that uses your brain is an intellectual pursuit. My mum was a primary-school dropout due to financial reasons after the war, but she has an incredibly sharp, active mind that has served her throughout her whole life and I see her as very intellectual, despite having zero qualifications.

Feeling doubtful about your intellectual prowess can have a real impact on your self-esteem, and in turn this impinges on your ability to make real connections with people, including partners. To tackle the issue of how intellect relates to relationships, let's look at the story of Tom and Sana, two clients of mine, whose names I've changed to protect their identity, as I have with all the case studies in this book.

HOW YOU FURNISH YOUR HOUSE

A Thirst for Knowledge

Tom grew up in Norway, a country where people are deemed to have a rather serious nature and Tom certainly fitted that stereotype. He came from a family who loved to talk about what some might deem 'intellectual' issues, deep into the night. When the long, snowy winters came, they would sometimes get holed-up for days in their mountain home, and the only thing left to do was bury their noses in a book. Consequently, their conversations revolved around their thoughts about the things they had read.

When he met Sana who fits within our 'tropical emotional type', he was attracted to her friendly nature and the fact that she loved to chat with him about her life and her feelings. After a few weeks however, Tom realised that Sana couldn't really hold a conversation with him, at least, on the level that he loved – what he would call an intellectual level. He got more and more frustrated as he felt that Sana wasn't his intellectual match, yet deep down he knew she was not a vacuous woman.

What Tom didn't realise was that the reason Sana didn't join in with his debates was because she was afraid of saying the wrong thing or even angering him with her opinions – she was not confident in her own intellectual capacities and so resorted to 'small talk'. This was because Sana had grown up with a father who was very strict, in fact, who would be considered abusive today for his behaviour. If she dared to contradict him she would be beaten with his belt. Also, her father would shout at her for being too noisy or talking too much. Subsequently, Sana, who was in awe of Tom's intelligence, felt frightened by his need to hear her opinion on everything. When they came to see me, I asked them both to look at how their respective upbringings had shaped their behaviour. Tom had to step back from constantly asking Sana for her opinion on everything and let her speak when she felt comfortable. He needed to let her feel like she would never be judged. Sana in turn had to understand that Tom loved reading and keeping himself abreast of current thinking, but that all he really wanted was to share knowledge with her, not to test her. Sana had to convince herself that Tom would never chide her for whatever opinion she had – that he was not her father – and that a debate was not a sign of anger.

Now, Tom is more relaxed and allows himself to laugh and joke like Sana, as well as discuss deeper issues. Sana has learnt to relax too and feel less defensive. She can listen to Tom sharing his new discovery or theory and finally contribute her opinions without feeling threatened.

HOW YOU FURNISH YOUR HOUSE

MAKE LOVE NOT WAR

Many people, like Sana, misinterpret an opposing view as an attack and because of this, it's all too easy to start a discussion and end up in a row. Even asking an innocuous question can end up in World War Three because the person's answer may come across as a personal slight, rather than simply their opinion. We are all so ready to take offence that a straightforward difference of opinion can become a minefield. It's neither right nor wrong to put the cream on a scone first, rather than the jam (which is a bone of contention between those living in Devon and their neighbours in Cornwall), but once someone has decided that your view threatens theirs, the atmosphere totally changes from a friendly chat into a frosty standoff or worse, a battle.

> *It's all too easy to start a discussion and end up in a row*

This is because emotions have got involved, muddying the clear waters of debate. In an ideal world, we should be able to explore an issue by taking a philosophical view, without hoping or needing to persuade the other person to agree with us. How often has a conversation descended into a bickering match about the tone of voice used, or worse, become a tit-for-tat about previous misdemeanours? When this happens, the main focus of the conversation is completely lost as emotional horns are locked and armour is donned. Very often these arguments can spin out of control and become serious, threatening the relationship itself, yet if you asked the individuals involved to step back and say what was at the root of the disagreement, very often, they couldn't say.

Using your intellect in these situations is a way to swerve around potentially explosive conversations. Staying cool and sticking to reason rather than rising to the bait of emotion, can help diffuse the tension. Does this seem a bit cold and calculating? When you consider the potential outcome, taking a breath and thinking of the rational approach works much better in the long run. Indeed, having the intellectual awareness that you don't always have to be right, and that differing views on certain subjects are healthy, can be a lifesaver, or at least a relationship-saver. An interesting article on the Forbes website[22] by Joseph Grenny, bestselling author of *Crucial Conversations*, suggests there are five mistakes we make during arguments, and five different strategies to avoid friction:

Mistake 1: Forgetting to phrase your words in a diplomatic way
When a conflict arises because someone has done something to annoy you, it's all too tempting to think that the only way to get your point across is to give it to them with both barrels, eg: "It's the millionth time that you've left your dirty underwear on the floor and I'm sick of living with a pig."

Strategy 1: Remember that it is possible to tell the truth without being hurtful
There's no need for brutal honesty because all that will happen is that the recipient will become defensive. We're always looking for the intent behind any interaction, and as soon as we perceive a threat, we batten down the hatches. As Grenny says: "It isn't the truth that hurts —

it's the malice used to deliver the truth." So, in the above example, your opening gambit could just present the facts: "Your clothes are on the floor."

Mistake 2: Thinking that you must share your feelings

Although I'm a great believer in expressing how you feel, there is a time and a place for everything, and during a delicate, potentially volatile situation it's best to keep things neutral. If you think about how the other person is going to process what you say, they're much more likely to react favourably if they haven't got the emotional weight of your feelings to deal with as well.

Strategy 2: Stick to the facts

Remember the reason behind your initial thought and follow that through, rather than focusing on the emotions associated with it. For example: "I would like you to put them in the washing basket," instead of: "You treat me like a servant." *Facts not feelings* is a mantra you need to remember when you're in an emotionally volatile situation. Our brains are hard-wired to remember emotions much more than facts, which is why when asked to be specific about a grievance, it's so hard to summon up examples. So before you wade-in to a sticky situation, step back, take a couple of slow, deep breaths and stick to the facts without introducing any emotional baggage.

Mistake 3: Going on the defensive

As mentioned before, we're trained to sniff out an attack like a bloodhound, so if there's any indication of a threat, in terms of body language or that the conversation is being hijacked by emotions, then we automatically become defensive, shoring up our own position in case we are attacked, even if only metaphorically. But when we go on the defensive, we barricade ourselves against what we perceive to be an onslaught – even if it is in reality an olive-branch of peace or an apology – we may not always see it.

Strategy 3: Have an enquiring mind
To avoid becoming defensive, or making others feel attacked, approach the situation with interest about the other person's perspective. Try to understand what has happened and see if there is a way to resolve it. In this case, by saying: "How do you think we could solve this problem? What would help remind you to put your clothes in the washing basket?" If someone feels understood, they are much more likely to be open to resolving the situation.

Mistake 4: Playing the blame game
When something is making you unhappy, it's very easy to apportion blame on others and feel righteous indignation about it – but where is this going to get you? If you blame someone for something they don't consider to be their fault, then all that will do is perpetuate bad feeling. Being diplomatic is far more affective because it keeps lines of negotiation open. Another important point to remember during conflict is that you may feel that you are entirely the innocent party, but try to be absolutely honest with yourself in understanding what part you have actually played.

Strategy 4: It takes two to tango
In other words, change your perspective. For example, is there a chance that you like to play the martyr, and that picking up the dirty underwear feeds your feelings of 'poor me,' making you feel self-righteous and indignant. Does this give you a feeling of importance in an otherwise

mundane situation? It's time to be brutally honest with yourself – it does take two to tango, so ask yourself if you could've avoided a fight by changing your perspective – not just about the underwear, but about your own levels of self-esteem, for example.

Mistake 5: Avoiding confrontation
Do you catastrophise about how a conversation is going to go, imagining the worst case scenario and then talking yourself out of addressing the issue at all? Don't worry, it's more common than you think, but retreating into silence is not helpful because you can't go through life side-stepping uncomfortable situations, because this just results in simmering resentment. You need to find a way to work through these situations in an intelligent way, sticking to the facts and thereby minimising any damage.

Strategy 5: Silence is deadly
Persuade yourself to articulate your thoughts in a calm, reasonable manner, by imagining the consequences if you don't. In this particular scenario, if you never pipe-up about his dirty boxer shorts, he will believe that you are not concerned where they land at the end of the day (or that the laundry fairy really does exist) and never know that he could make you so happy with just the tiny amount of effort it takes to put them in the washing basket. Genny suggests the order of your thoughts should be: firstly imagine what would happen if you didn't say anything; secondly, imagine what would happen if you did and things went well; and thirdly imagine if the conversation backfires and how you will deal with that, calmly and rationally. Apparently, using this thought process allows you to broach the subject whilst having all likely outcomes covered, so that you can stay calm

and achieve your goal of 'pants in the basket'. Remember too, the imaginative goal setting that creates new neural pathways, as we discussed in Chapter One, which will be incredibly helpful in this respect.

Couples often find themselves in a row because they expect different things from a conversation. "Does my bum look big in this?" never, never, EVER warrants the reply, "Yes." The woman (I'm assuming, though it could also be a man) just needs reassurance that she looks okay. Equally, being asked, "What's wrong?" is a minefield that can easily be navigated. Don't reply: "Nothing," just because you feel angry that they don't already know. Men (and again, I'm making an assumption here, it could be a woman with a male-type brain) aren't mind readers, and they can be less intuitive than women, so cut them some slack – that is, use your intellect rather than your emotions – and answer honestly. If you do this, over time he will get better at predicting the reason for your unhappiness and harmony will be restored.

A really thought-provoking viral blog post on this subject is *She Divorced Me Because I Left Dishes by the Sink*[23], in which the blogger, Matt, reflects on his failed marriage. It's the perfect example of using rational, intellectual reasoning to solve a problem, unfortunately for Matt, a little too late. During his marriage, he repeatedly ignored his wife's request to put dirty glasses in the dishwasher, instead leaving them on the worktop, arguing that it didn't bother him so why does it matter? His arguments ran along the lines of: *I may want to use it again; I'll do it if guests are coming over; Is it really that important?* He couldn't understand why she didn't feel the same way. This lack of respect for her feelings eroded her love for him until she eventually left him.

At first, he couldn't understand why something so trivial could end their relationship, but with the clear-eyed rational thinking that only comes with hindsight, he gradually came to realise that it wasn't the glass that was the issue, it was his lack of consideration for her, particularly her perspective (see strategy 4, above). *He* didn't care about the glass, but *she* did and that is what he should've focused on: he should've changed his perspective. Too late, he realised that he should have applied his intellect to the situation and employed diplomacy and negotiation, rather than digging his heels in and feeling got at. The emotional charge became so great that he totally lost sight of what was important: that he loved her and wanted to make her happy; his actions were saying the opposite. To put it another way, he was cutting off his nose to spite his face – something he later admits.

The power of thinking: "S/he doesn't feel how I feel on this issue, and I need to accept that and act accordingly, not hope to change him/her," is monumental – a mighty piece of rationalism that is often overlooked in the hothouse environment of a relationship.

Margaret and Andrew's story that follows is another example of what can happen when a relationship is thwarted by opposing perspectives.

The Pressure to Perform

Margaret was studying at university in the early 90s when she met Andrew, who worked at the local bar. He was a student himself but enjoyed chatting to customers more than studying. She found him refreshing and a great distraction from her college books, and so started their relationship. Andrew dropped out of uni eventually and worked full time at the bar while she continued with her studies. Margaret managed to secure an amazing job with her specialised skills and they moved to a bigger city.

When she fell pregnant with their first baby, the decision was made for Andrew to stay at home to look after the baby as he was in a less well-paid job. Soon after, Margaret was offered an interesting post, which meant moving to the US. By then, Andrew had become what's known in the ex-pat community as 'the trailing spouse' (following your partner wherever the job takes them) and was the stay-at-home parent. Two more children and many countries later, he still didn't have a career and she was the main income earner. Margaret knew that his confidence had been knocked by this and was always encouraging him to try and find something that interested him, and that could earn him some money. As the years passed, Margaret became more exasperated with Andrew's lack of motivation to better himself while she was constantly going on courses to keep her expertise relevant to her work. She knew he loved writing and had written some poetry in the past so she sent him off on a writing retreat for his 40th birthday, hoping that it would kick start his enthusiasm again. It did… For all of two months.

Margaret started to realise that whilst she had pushed herself and used her intellect to its full potential, Andrew was stuck in a rut and yet was unwilling to do anything about it. In turn, Andrew felt pressurised to be something he wasn't and consequently felt inadequate. When they discussed the issue, Andrew insisted that he was happy with the status quo of being the stay-at-home spouse, despite the fact that he often moaned to friends about wanting to achieve things in his life besides being the father of three children.

Eventually Margaret came to understand that Andrew was actually happy in his role as 'martyr' and really had no intention of changing, preferring to stay in his comfort zone and complain about it. Whatever she said or did, she couldn't transform him into the happy, fulfilled person that she wanted him to be and she realised that their intellectual incompatibility – or at least his refusal to meet her half way – was a big deal for her. They decided to go their separate ways by their 20th wedding anniversary.

On the one hand, it's heartening that Margaret had the vision to see that it was fruitless trying to get Andrew to better himself, because *nobody can make their partner change if they don't want to*. But on the other, how sad for Andrew to be rejected largely due to his resistance and fear of stepping outside his comfort zone to reach his full potential? If Andrew's experience hits a nerve with you, don't worry, because the realisation that things need to change can be all that is necessary to get motivated. Andrew's problem was that he was resistant to change, and perhaps that he liked his comfort zone more than his relationship.

> *Nobody can make their partner change if they don't want to*

Before we continue to explore how engaging meaningfully with your partner is possible, I just wanted to reassure any stay-at-home parents. I am not saying that caring for your children full-time is not a valid, valuable or rewarding occupation (as I know only too well, having four children myself), but it can also be mind-numbing and thankless. Also, as it is not a high-status occupation – although it should be, it's hard enough! You don't get social recognition and appreciation for it, which everyone craves. Therefore, making sure that you have a wide variety of interests that stimulate you, gets you out of the house and fires-up those brain cells during the precious time you have to yourself, is essential.

Whether you work in the home or outside it, there are huge benefits to flexing your intellectual muscles on a regular basis, such as:
- It helps you feel good about yourself
- It helps you connect with other people
- It helps you find a partner

On the Same Page

A fascinating article by dating expert Christie Hartman[24] shows how having an intellectual connection with someone is an important element of a relationship. After the honeymoon period is over, when the physical spark that drew you together is not burning quite as brightly, you need a basic compatibility that keeps you interesting to each other. Being able to have a conversation on a subject that delves a little deeper than: "What's for dinner?" is a good start. Hartman goes on to explain that being 'on the same page' intellectually can be vital to the relationship. (Like me, she draws the distinction between academic qualifications and intellect.)

> *Being able to have a conversation on a subject that delves a little deeper than: "What's for dinner?" is a good start.*

From my own experience, I have learnt how important it is to be able to engage with your partner on a cerebral level. When my husband and I started dating, I wanted to make sure that he and I were on the same page. Even though I didn't have a university degree at that time, I knew that I was smart enough to match up intellectually to his double-degree mind. As a bit of fun, I suggested we did a Mensa-type IQ test online. I scored 140 and he got 139. This was so gratifying to me and we laughed about it! We talked about how I would have completed my Master's degree, had my financial situation at the time allowed it. We discussed how we both love reading non-fiction books; he likes autobiographies, history and science and I like psychology and self-improvement. When it comes to fiction, our shared love is for thrillers and we exchanged books by the likes of Stephen King, James Patterson, Robin Cook and Patricia Cornwell. He also highly recommended Jean M. Auel's book, *Clan of the Cave Bear*, which ultimately led me to fine-tuning my coaching style.

After we got married, he encouraged me to complete my education so that I could fulfil my potential. I got to the point where I was taking one diploma after another! Equally, he made sure that his professional knowledge base was up to scratch by upgrading his skills in clinical data. Because of our mutual thirst for knowledge, we would talk over dinner, sharing what we'd learnt that day in such a way that each could fully appreciate what the other was saying, without feeling overwhelmed or intimidated. We would give opinions about each other's work and provide a different perspective whilst still accepting our differences of opinion. We never think in terms of one of us being superior to the other, just different. Of course it's not all roses, and like every other couple under the sun, we have the odd tiff or misunderstanding, but I really do think that being genuinely fascinated in each other's interests has been vital to our marriage over the years.

Allowing my intellectual side to blossom has been valuable in two ways: it has boosted my self-esteem to discover that I can hold my own in lofty conversations, and it has also enabled a deeper connection with my partner, who admires and respects my new-found cognitive abilities.

It's a win-win, and something I encourage you to pursue for yourself with future partners. I think it's fair to say that you get out of a relationship what you put in. If you don't water the seeds of your relationship, it will wither and die; but if you do, it will flourish and bloom. This wasn't always possible, as traditionally, marriages were based on economic and social foundations with the woman being very much secondary to the man, and expected to know her place (in the kitchen). Now, thanks to universal suffrage, the feminist movement and improving equality in the work place, women have become more vocal about what they need in a relationship. As a result, relationships have moved from being economically motivated to being more person-centred – that is, how the partner can satisfy an intellectual, not just an economic need.

Research at Monmouth University in New Jersey[25] has studied how we use relationships to accumulate knowledge and experiences, that researchers call 'self-expansion'. Similar to what I discovered during the early years of my marriage, the results of the study revealed that that the more self-expansion people experience from their partner, the more committed and satisfied they are in the relationship. Although this can sound self-serving, as if you're only in the relationship for what you can get out of it, it works both ways. The reward and satisfaction of encouraging your partner to expand their horizons also reaps dividends as it can lead to stronger, more sustainable relationships. As leader of the study, Dr Lewandowski says: "If you're seeking self-growth and obtain it from your partner, then that puts your partner in a pretty important position. And being able to help your partner's self-expansion would be pretty pleasing to yourself."

Being in this type of nurturing relationship also reveals to you new aspects of your personality that you didn't know existed. For example, if you didn't consider yourself to have a particularly good sense of humour but your partner roars at your jokes, you'll come to realise that yes, actually you are funny. It can be so healing to discover the traits that perhaps had been squashed out of you during childhood – either from critical parents or even negative schoolteachers – can once again flourish within a supportive relationship.

Now, if you're currently single, I bet you're wondering how all this applies to you, since it's concerning relationships, the very thing that you're hoping for but haven't yet got. Well, the fact is that even when looking for a partner, how you use your intellect is relevant. Biological anthropologist Dr Helen Fisher[26] found that experts in the field of human relationships couldn't agree on what drives attraction – is it true what they say? Do opposites attract or are you more likely to gravitate to someone who shares your personality traits? So in search of an answer herself, she used biology to investigate further. Based on the neurochemical systems in our brains, Dr Fisher identified four broad styles of thinking and then went on to study how these affect who you choose as a partner and which are the most compatible for you in the longer term. See if you can recognise yourself in them.

Explorer

This type of person looks out, not in. They crave novelty, new experiences and seek adventures. They are susceptible to boredom, can be energetic and enthusiastic. They can also be intellectually curious, mentally flexible and creative. Dr Fisher describes this style of thinking as 'curious/energetic'. On a neuroscientific level, the relevant brain chemical associated with these traits is dopamine.

Builder

The builder is someone who is sociable, cautious, less anxious and develops close friendships. They tend to follow social norms, abide by the rules and respect authority. They're self-controlled, precise, conscientious and have an interest in details. In Dr Fisher's categorisation, they're dubbed: 'Cautious/social-norm compliant' and the brain chemical linked with them is serotonin.

Director

An interesting mix of self-confidence, assertiveness and acute attention to detail describe the director personality type. They often have enhanced visual-spatial perception and work in computers, maths, engineering or music – something that uses rule-based systems. Often less socially aware, they can be emotionally contained. Dr Fisher calls this temperament 'Analytical/tough-minded' and it's linked with testosterone.

Negotiator

The negotiator is articulate, intuitive, empathetic and nurturing. Often generous and trusting, the negotiator longs to make social attachments and has a heightened memory for emotional experiences. They also have keen imaginations and are mentally flexible, often seeing the bigger picture. In Dr Fisher's categorisation, people with this group of traits are called 'prosocial/empathetic' and are associated with oestrogen.

It's fascinating to think how the particular chemical cocktail in our brains explains our personalities. After identifying these four types, to explore her theory in practise, Fisher then worked with the dating website www.chemistry.com

to anonymously interview people about their personality and dating preferences. Fisher knew that people often make up their minds about a potential partner as early as during the initial 'getting-to-know-you' conversations from research by Sunnafrank and Ramirez[27], so a dating website was a good place to start.

After observing who approached who and why (and this element of the study must have been great fun, watching all that online flirting going on) Fisher discovered that both the theories: 'opposites attract' *and* 'like attracts like' are true – *but only with certain categories*. In other words, the adventurous and bold explorers were likely to be drawn to similar types, as were the conventional and rule-abiding builders, but the assertive directors are more likely to plump for the nurturing negotiators and vice versa. See below to find out why.

Happy matches

Explorer + explorer
This unconventional, flexible pair, seize the day together in search of new adventures. Because of their low boredom threshold, the partnership may have a short shelf life as they go in search of new excitement, but Fisher argues this is still a biologically favourable strategy because a series of partnerships produces more varied young. Sounds a bit chilly and not exactly romantic, but if both of you are serial monogamists then you'll have the same mind set about relationships and are likely to be less heartbroken when it's over.

Builder + builder
Calm, precise and loyal, builders capitalise on their shared strengths to form a strong relationship. Rarely impulsive

with money, actions or feelings, they provide a solid and predictable foundation for each other, which is wonderful as builders thrive on stability. Because of this, they're willing to overlook differences to make the relationship last but on the downside, they can be moralistic and critical, digging their heels in when they think they're right.

Director і negotiator
At first sight, these are very different types of people, but on closer examination you can see that they are both comfortable with abstract thinking; one focuses on details whilst the other looks at the bigger picture. This means that as a partnership, they are likely to make decisions together well. The negotiator appreciates the director's plain-speaking and focus whilst the director needs the negotiator's empathy and people skills. Problems occur when the director's insensitivity tramples on the negotiator's feelings or the negotiator's emotional openness grates on the director's nerves.

Other combinations are, of course, possible but Dr Fisher is examining who is naturally drawn to each other, due to the chemical makeup of their brains. If you can identify with any of these personality types (or even recognise pairings in friends and family – I certainly can!) then you can use them to understand why a certain personality type would work better for you. For example, if you're a sensitive, nurturing negotiator, it's best to steer clear of those explorers who won't appreciate your intuition and get impatient with your hesitance to make a decision.

This is how you apply your intellect to choosing a potential partner – all very cool and rational, but what about when you fancy the pants off someone who is intellectually incompatible? What do you do then? An insightful article on the Futurescopes website[28] says there are several ways around it. First you need to decide how important an intellectual connection is to you – perhaps you just love the socks off them even though they don't share your passion for literature. But if you think this may be a stumbling block, you could try gently encouraging them to broaden their perspectives. Alternatively, you could accept that you don't look to your relationship for providing intellectual stimulation and seek it outside the relationship, at a book club or news forum, for example. Discover what happened to Gino when he met his intellectual match.

HOW YOU FURNISH YOUR HOUSE

Appearances Can Be Deceptive

Gino's relationship history was pretty chequered. He had been a playboy in his native New York and was generally more comfortable with one-night stands and casual affairs rather than anything serious. He usually ended the flings, ironically because he was afraid to be alone; he was so fearful of rejection that he got in there first. One woman, Tammy, turned his head because of her forceful personality, which reminded him of his strong, independent mother.

After their marriage, Tammy was happy just spending his money and focusing on looking good – her only reading material being celebrity magazines. Gino felt frustrated because as a successful banker, travelling around the world hobnobbing with politicians, he wanted to be able to discuss his work with her – but she wasn't receptive to this. He realised that her strength of character wasn't matched by her intellect. Ultimately, Gino lost respect for her because she didn't share his interests and they separated. In terms of the intellectual types we have discussed above, I would say that Gino was an explorer and Tammy was a builder – ultimately, not very compatible.

Gino then went on to meet Katrina, who had travelled extensively due to being a TCK (Third Culture Kid – children raised in a country other than their parents'). When I spoke with Gino about him falling in love with Katrina, he told me he was afraid of the feelings he had for her. This was the first time he'd really understood what falling in love means. He was initially worried that he and Katrina were intellectually incompatible as she was much younger and was happy working as a waitress while waiting for her Green Card. Yet as their relationship developed, he realised that she was perfectly capable of holding her own in any discussions they had.

Gino saw how rational and logical Katrina was during these conversations and she could support her argument with facts, some of which he himself had shared with her months ago. Gino realised that intellectual compatibility had nothing to do with similar educational standards, but was more a meeting of minds and a sharing of interests. In terms of their intellect, I would say that to compliment Gino's explorer type, Katrina has a negotiator type, where she is happy to be flexible, empathetic and can see the bigger picture regarding what makes their relationship work.

Gino and Katrina are now enjoying reading up about the various places and cultures they want to travel to together. Their intellectual compatibility has provided firm foundations for them to share their life experiences.

Through the Key Hole

Now we've examined the part our intellects play in our social and romantic lives, let's return to our house metaphor. To my mind, the hard furnishings of anyone's ideal home say a lot about them as a person. I have a friend who loves to cook on an Aga, a slow-oven that gently works its magic, and heats the whole house too. I would say my friend's intellectual type is a builder: he is calm yet cautious, initially quite wary of strangers, but once accepted you are welcomed warmly into his home. I have another friend whose love of the sleek, modern bathroom has taken 'contemporary' to new heights. Her showerhead is the size of a dustbin lid, and there's a huge Buddha statue at the end of the shower room – something that would slightly unnerve me if I had to undress in front of it! She has wall-to-wall mirrors with a bronzed tone and a sun-pipe that lets natural light in. Her bathroom is like one you'd find in a high-end villa in Bali, and her tastes are eclectic. It probably wouldn't surprise you if I said her intellect type was director.

I'd like you to now have a think through how your intellect was nurtured in your childhood and what impact this has had on your relationships. Once again, make sure you have around 20 minutes of uninterrupted time so you can devote your whole attention to this exercise.

THE ARCHITECT OF LOVE

1. Thinking back to your childhood, what did it feel like to live in your parental home? Was there warmth and comfort, love and encouragement, or was it a cold and rigid life where you felt unable to express your true feelings? Your answers translate to how your intellect was formed and encouraged (or not), and how receptive this makes you to new challenges.

_____
_____
_____
_____
_____
_____
_____
_____
_____
_____
_____
_____
_____
_____
_____
_____
_____
_____
_____
_____
_____
_____
_____

HOW YOU FURNISH YOUR HOUSE

2. Now think about your own home. Is it similar in any way to your parental home? Do you reflect their values, or have you created a new environment from which you function more fully? This will help you to understand how you absorb intellectual information and whether you are traditional and prefer to conform or seek out new experiences and take unconventional learning paths. Remember, there is no right or wrong answer, rather, view it as a glimpse inside your psyche and try to interpret your answers as a way of gaining an insight into your intellect.

_____
_____
_____
_____
_____
_____
_____
_____
_____
_____
_____
_____
_____
_____
_____
_____
_____
_____
_____
_____
_____
_____
_____

3. How has your intellect helped you thus far? Do you exercise your intellectual muscles, or are you more of an emotional being? Can you see an opportunity to improve your intellectual capacities at all? Now take a look at the intellectual archetypes above. Are you naturally an explorer? Or do you see yourself as having elements of different archetypes?

_____
_____
_____
_____
_____
_____
_____
_____
_____
_____
_____
_____
_____
_____
_____
_____
_____
_____
_____
_____
_____
_____
_____
_____

HOW YOU FURNISH YOUR HOUSE

4. How do you communicate your thoughts? Are you able to successfully translate your thoughts and feelings into words? Or do you get frustrated that people never understand you properly? Identifying your strengths and weaknesses in this area will help you crystalise who you are as a person.

THE ARCHITECT OF LOVE

5. Where do you consider yourself to be now in your intellectual life? Do you have a stimulating career? Are your hobbies fulfilling? Do you stretch and challenge yourself intellectually? Consider your answers and then plan how your intellect could play a more prominent role in your life. Remember, like furniture that gets dusty over time, your intellect needs the occasional polish. Imagine those trusty kitchen cabinets that have stored your food for so many years. Couldn't they do with an upgrade, new handles, a lick of paint perhaps? Equally, upgrading your own mental faculties and keeping them fully functioning can boost your self-esteem, your communication skills and your future relationships.

_____
_____
_____
_____
_____
_____
_____
_____
_____
_____
_____
_____
_____
_____
_____
_____
_____
_____
_____
_____

CHAPTER FOUR

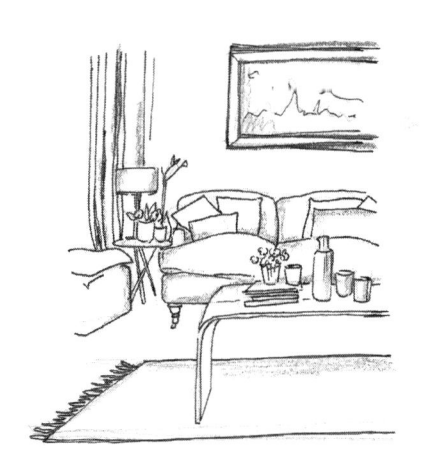

KNOWING WHAT YOU WANT

Soft Furnishings and Sexuality

What's the difference between a house and a home? A house serves a purpose, it's a functional building that fulfils your need for shelter, but a home carries with it a lot more emotional weight. After all, in *The Wizard of Oz*, Dorothy doesn't say: "There's no place like house," does she! Home is where you feel safe and warm, where you can fully be yourself without judgement. Many of the cosy things we surround ourselves with in our homes – rugs, cushions, throws – go towards making a house feel like a home. These soft furnishings transform a barren shell into an inviting den. They're what we need to help us truly relax, to feel comfortable in our skins. What we choose, from Persian rugs to rattan blinds, suggests how contented we are with our sensual selves. This is why I see the soft furnishings in our dream homes as equating to our sexual nature.

Whilst I understand that some people find interior design far more fascinating than others, and a bachelor flat may be less inviting than a marital home, nonetheless, an examination of our *preferences* – whether for warm colours, sumptuous rugs and candlelight or muted tones, wooden floors and natural lighting – is very revealing. What we are drawn to reflects who we are, and so it is your preferences that I want you to think about, even if your own home, for whatever reason, doesn't necessarily showcase them.

Before we delve into this fascinating arena, I would like to flag up an important point. It's natural to bring your own assumptions about sexuality with you when you read this chapter, but I want to remind you that just as we are all different people, we all have different views on sexuality – both what we think is 'normal' and what works for us on a personal level. I hope to reach out to everyone, regardless of their particular preferences, and this means the lesbian, gay, bisexual, transgender and queer communities (LGBTQ), as well as people with low and high libidos, single, married, divorced; in short, this chapter is relevant to everyone. I also want to acknowledge the large swathes of the world where people are expected to stay a virgin until marriage. As a result, I'm taking a much wider view on sexuality than many will expect. For all of you out there who think we're going to plunge into a world of hardcore titillation, think again. I'm interested in the whole gamut, including sensuality, flirting and affection. This, to me, comes under the umbrella term of sexuality.

An interesting article in *Psychology Today*[29] makes the same point: "Is a couple 'having sex' if they engage in some other form of intercourse, such as oral or anal? What if they are having some other form of sex such as rubbing against one another, any part against any part, which is pleasurable and can result in orgasm to either or both? Isn't that sex too? It is in my book. Perhaps the question might be recast as how important is orgasm or even, how important is pleasurable and intimate touch?"

I particularly like that last point: that pleasurable touch can be classed as sexual, so that includes massage and cuddling. Whilst some people (I hesitate to say men, but it's often the case) are blessed with a libido that can be switched on like a lightbulb, others (yes ditto, women) need more warming-up. To continue the metaphor, if stereotypical male libido is like a lightbulb, typically, female sexuality is like a real fire; lots of preparation and careful attention is required until finally you're rewarded with a roaring blaze that heats up the whole house.

> *If stereotypical male libido is like a lightbulb, female sexuality is like a real fire*

I've heard about a massage service aimed directly at women in which a male masseur incorporates sexual touch to enable the woman to climax. Initially, this sounds just like the female equivalent of those dubious massage parlours that promise a 'happy ending', but the key difference here is that it specifically aims to make the woman feel confident, unashamed and unrepressed about her body.

Many women (and some men) find it hard to reach orgasm, and the fact that this type of massage exists suggests that they need taking by the hand (forgive me!) and gently guiding towards sexual release, almost to be given permission to climax, which actually makes it quite poignant and a sorry reflection of our cultural heritage. Whilst in Scandinavian and Northern European countries, sex education is an integral part of education as a whole, and is taught in a way that makes children feel open and relaxed about discussing it (and as a consequence, they have one of the lowest rates of teenage pregnancy), other cultures associate sex with shame and embarrassment. I truly believe that our sensual selves are a vital part of who we are and should not be hidden away and never spoken of.

The impact that repressed, conservative views on sex has on a population is never clearer than in Malaysia. This country, neighbouring my native Singapore, is mostly secular, apart from the state of Kelantan and a few other east coast cities, which have very strict religious laws. Here, there is a very conservative attitude to sex, including sex education, but ironically, where watching internet porn is concerned, these places occupy the top two spots.[30] The same correlation has been found in many cities in other countries – the more adherence to religion, the more porn is watched. So it goes to show that all attempts to control and limit sexual activity only serve to make people find an outlet elsewhere. Unfortunately, internet porn as a source of education and stimulation just gives people an unrealistic view of sex. If we have a relaxed, open and straightforward attitude to talking about sex, then we're much more likely to be confident and secure about what we want in our sex lives.

When I was running a course called 'Connecting with your Inner Goddess' I mentioned the importance of knowing your body intimately and what gives you pleasure. This included a discussion of masturbation and the class' reaction was priceless. Open-mouths and blushes all round. I understand that we have been brought up to see masturbation as taboo, but how else can you discover what turns you on? How else are you going to find out that a particular spot on your neck is delightfully sensitive other than with a thorough investigation of your body? And if you don't know yourself intimately, how are you going to communicate what you want to a partner? Ultimately, this is the key to a happy sex life. If you are a happy to touch your own body, to pleasure yourself, then you are comfortable with your own sensuality. This works in your favour in two ways: Firstly, educating yourself about your likes and dislikes helps to improve your sex life and secondly, being in touch with your sensual side is extremely attractive to potential soulmates.

> *If you don't know yourself intimately, how are you going to communicate what you want to a partner?*

As little children, we instinctively play with our bodies, just because it feels good, and this natural habit is scolded out of us until we associate masturbation with shame. In some cultures, people are so alienated from their own bodies that they find it difficult to use the correct terms for their genitals, preferring silly terms instead of vagina and penis, even as adults. I think using the correct, scientific names for our genitals is a good way of normalising what are just parts of our body.

Whilst we're on the subject of normalisation, one of the biggest fears around sexuality is worrying about what is normal. What is the normal amount of times to have sex per week? Is it normal to be attracted to the same sex? Or even, am I abnormal for wanting something different in the bedroom? There is a huge fear associated with not being seen as 'normal'. The increasingly sexualised images on TV and in the media exacerbate this fear. "I can't possibly compete with him/her – I'm not sexy enough," we think, when watching glamorous film stars. The media also shines the spotlight on their relationships, so that they're forced to gush about how in love they are with their partner, never mentioning the fact that he's so grumpy in the mornings or she's unbearable when she's got PMT.

We create this unrealistic image of their lives and it is only when they split up that we're reassured that despite their glittering facade, they're human after all. I actually find it heartening when famous couples have long, successful relationships – David Bowie (may he rest in peace) and wife Iman, for instance. In an interview with *The Guardian* in 2014[31], Iman was refreshingly grounded about the reality of their relationship: "I fell in love with David Jones. I did not fall in love with David Bowie. Bowie is just a persona." To me, Iman's down-to-earth attitude – that she fell in love with an ordinary man – is refreshing: look beyond the façade that first attracts you, to find the real person within. That's what we're aiming to do in this book.

> *Everything is normal for you*

As they say, 'Comparison is the thief of joy', which we'd all do well to remember when thinking about our sex lives. Is it more normal to have sex all the time or once in a blue moon? If 3% of us have sex every day[32] does that makes the rest of us feel inadequate? The same figure has sex just once a year. Are we supposed to feel superior now? The answer is that whether you're very sexually active, hardly at all or even a virgin, everything is normal *for you*. The pressure to fit into an idealised notion of a conventional relationship is enormous, and we need to remember that it's nonsense. We should only do what we're comfortable with, which reminds me of Johan and Lily's story, below.

Be True To Yourself

Johan's parents worshipped him, and as they were from a traditional Asian culture, they expected him to follow in their footsteps – meet a nice girl, marry and have children. For years, he intended to fulfil their expectations but somehow found it hard to commit to serious relationships. Then he met Lily. She was wonderful: funny, friendly and they got on like a house on fire. Johan's parents were delighted – finally he had met someone who he could settle down with.

Lily was over the moon too, and was willing to take things further in their relationship – a big step considering sex outside marriage was forbidden in their culture. Yet when it came to the moment when their relationship could turn sexual, Johan felt repulsed. Imagining being intimate with her disgusted him. One of the most natural things in the world went against how he felt deep inside. Johan admitted to Lily something that he had known in his heart for a long time: that he was not sexually attracted to women, but to men. He was gay and he knew that he could not continue with the relationship.

Initially, everyone was devastated. Lily adored him and the rejection was painful. His parents were shocked that their perfect son was homosexual and the life they'd anticipated for him would never be a reality. Not to mention the public shame in their culture, which wasn't accepting of homosexuality.

Eventually, after months and years, everyone began to accept that Johan's decision had been the right one. Lily would have had a life of heartbreak being

KNOWING WHAT YOU WANT

with a man who did not find her physically attractive and Johan would not have been true to himself. Lily went on to meet someone who adored her on every level and Johan moved to a big city to discover his own sexuality, with the support of his family. Johan was happier than he'd been in a long time now he could finally reveal who he really was

Johan's courage to face up to his innermost desires is admirable. Too many people are living a lie, simply because what they truly want is frowned upon, socially or culturally. So long as it's not harming anyone, I say go for what makes you happy. Your self-belief and confidence will shine out, attracting admiration from all around you.

The Secret to Amazing Foreplay

I've got your attention now haven't I? But it's not what you think. Instead of a tip from *Cosmopolitan* magazine that may or may not work, the secret I'm referring to is communication, specifically listening. As Edward de Bono[33] said: "There is nothing more appealing than a good listener. A good listener is very nearly as attractive as a good talker. You cannot have a beautiful mind if you do not know how to listen."

I am a naturally chatty, friendly person and I find that men seem to be drawn to me, even when I'm not trying to get their attention. I'm often cheekily asked out for dates and in reply I show them my wedding ring. "I should've known you'd be married! Have you got a single friend just like you?" they exclaim. For some time I pondered upon why this was – why did these men find me attractive? Then it came to me: all I do is ask them questions and listen to the answers. For a brief moment, I make them the centre of attention, and they're enveloped in a warm blanket of feeling special. This harmless flirting gives both parties an enormous boost. You make them feel good then bathe in the reflected glow. Engaging with someone in a playful, cheeky way is a wonderful way to interact – bypassing the dull, "what do you do?", "where do you live?" questions, instead asking them something ticklish that provokes a funny reply.

An article on the website Limitless (lmt-lss.com)[34] makes a great point about the link between conversation and foreplay. "Conversation helps you open up to each other and goes above and beyond just being attracted to each other's appearance. It unlocks your ability to be vulnerable before each other and foreplay is probably one of the most vulnerable things on the planet after sex. Making conversation is an intimate and personal act."

Relationships are all about give and take, and if you can start out on the right foot at the beginning, you're more likely to achieve lasting happiness. Talking openly and honestly and listening closely are more effective aphrodisiacs than oysters and champagne put together.

You may think that when you've achieved your dream of finding a partner, you can relax, but no, please don't. Remind them frequently of the person you were when they met you – super-keen, enthusiastic and excited to be with them. Obviously, the ups and downs of every relationship can make this difficult, but never lose sight of why you were attracted to them, and why they found you attractive. I'd also recommend trying to keep that sensual light alive – your libido needs a little encouragement sometimes, or it can start to wane. The more often you have sex, the more often you're likely to feel in the mood.

> *Making conversation is an intimate and personal act*

A couple that I worked with, Björn and Shamini, went through a bumpy patch in their marriage when the lines of communication broke down. Discover how they managed to get over it.

Talk To Me

From the first day they met, Bjorn and Shamini had always been open with each other and as a result, their relationship was very happy. They each knew what the other wanted and worked hard to make one another feel loved. They'd met in the United States and when Bjorn was offered a job back in his native Sweden, he proposed to Shamini so she could return with him. Shamini felt confident that they would be happy anywhere they lived and agreed to marry him.

At first, their new life together in Sweden was blissful, but when Shamini gave birth to their first baby, their previously solid marriage started to show cracks. Shamini developed post-natal depression and all she did was sleep, cry and breastfeed. She withdrew from Bjorn and was locked into her own little world of unhappiness. As she had moved away from her family to be with Bjorn, she was completely isolated. Normally, all the female relatives in her community would rally around and help a new mother, especially if she was suffering from post-natal depression, but she didn't have that support network to rely on and instead just turned in on herself.

Sex was the last thing on her mind and Bjorn felt sidelined. He couldn't understand what had happened to his fun-loving Shamini. She had stopped communicating with him, stopped being intimate in any way, let alone sexually. Bjorn realised that their marriage was in crisis and sat Shamini down. "Talk to me," he said. "I don't know what's happening with you."

KNOWING WHAT YOU WANT

Shamini broke down in tears and explained that in the depths of her misery, she had lost sight of what was important – communicating her feelings. She no longer felt like a woman, a wife, instead being a mother had totally consumed her. Bjorn felt so relieved that she felt able to reach out to him that he wept too. They slowly pieced back together their former relationship. Shamini still felt too fragile to completely return to her sex life, but she was happy to satisfy Bjorn in other ways.

Your soul mate should be the one person you can be totally honest with, about all your wishes, dreams, fears and insecurities. You should feel accepted for who you are and in return, be receptive to their wants and needs, not just in bed but everywhere.

When times are tough, like they were for Shamini, your libido takes a knock, but this is the time to open up and confess your worries to your partner, rather than shut down and stop communicating. That is the only way that your soulmate can help you recover from your emotional dip and in turn help your sex-drive recover.

Sex and sensuality needn't just be about fulfilling a physical need, it can also be a very healing, nurturing experience. Many years ago, I was in a toxic relationship that left me at a very low ebb. The next person I had a physical connection with didn't develop into a relationship – firstly because it was on the rebound, and therefore didn't have a long sell-by date, and secondly because I knew he would always be a 'friend with benefits', but he was the best thing that could have happened to me at that time. He was very loving, calm, discreet and made me feel attractive once again.

After being told that I was fat and ugly by my ex, my self-esteem was at rock bottom but he persuaded me that I wasn't. He took a photo of me and said: "Look, this proves you're beautiful." His gentleness and sensitivity completely healed the wounds caused by the previous relationship, leaving me ready to meet someone new. Feeling like an alluring, sensual person is incredibly powerful, and sends out signals to the world that you're an attractive proposition. This is why it's so important to take care of your sexual self-esteem.

When Is It Okay To Compromise?

Having a satisfying sex life is all about being playful, open and uninhibited. For me and my husband, laughing in the bedroom is the way we express our sensuality. I can pinpoint the conception of our children to the times when we had a fit of the giggles. (Which contradicts Woody Allen's famous quote: "Sex is the most fun you can have without laughing," but anyway…) Obviously, given that most people have busy lives and are juggling hundreds of different demands on their time, you can't always expect the sexual Olympics – when you're tired and it's late, conventional or 'vanilla' sex is the obvious choice but sometimes you might fancy chocolate body butter!

Experimenting is great fun, and a good way to keep your relationship fresh, but how would you feel if your partner suggests something you're not sure about? Are you willing to step outside your sexual comfort zone? A while ago I joined an LGBTQ forum, in the hope of striking up a friendship with a gay man (I am interested to learn more about the LGBTQ lives and community) and during my visits there, I got chatting with a heterosexual woman who was looking for a bisexual encounter. She confessed to me that she felt very unsure about this and was only going along with her partner's wishes. It was his fantasy to have a threesome with two women, and because she wanted to please him, she was willing to try it even though she didn't like the idea. To me, this relationship had entered the danger zone. It had gone from 'healthily experimental' to 'toxic and coercive'. I suggested to her that it was more important to look after her own feelings and to only agree to a new sexual activity if she was totally happy with it.

Ask yourself – what am I willing to try, in the context of a loving relationship? What am I comfortable with and what are my absolute no-nos? If you don't believe in sex before marriage but your new partner is keen to consummate the relationship, will you put your foot down or are you happy to compromise your values for him/her? Establish your sexual parameters.

However, if you find yourself in a situation where you and your partner's fantasies aren't compatible, it doesn't necessarily signal the end of the relationship. There are ways around it that can still please both parties. For example, if your partner confesses that he/she craves the excitement of a one-night stand, instead of agreeing to an open relationship, you could instead suggest trying role play, where you arrange to meet at a new café/bar, instead of your usual favourite, and pretend to be on a blind date. Alternatively, if you want to try bondage and your partner isn't keen, you could watch an erotic film together with this subject matter, such as *Fifty Shades of Grey*. Getting creative and thinking laterally could enable you both to share and act on your most intimate desires without having to compromise your feelings.

The key here, once again, is communication. It's embarrassing talking about sex, especially if you're worried that your partner may blow a gasket at your suggestion, but it's essential. I advocate an actually quite unromantic attitude to discussing this subject – if you're clear about what you want, then it's easier to avoid the problem that Frank and Rebecca found themselves with.

Unhappily Ever After?

On paper, Frank and Rebecca's relationship was perfect. They were both attractive and successful people who had been together for 10 years and were still in love with each other. But scratch the surface and you find a very different picture. When they first met, Rebecca was enthusiastic in the bedroom and Frank took that to mean that her libido was the same as his, but as the months went by, he began to notice that they were having sex much less often than he would have liked. Any sexual advances he made were gently rebuffed until he gave up and tried to be satisfied with the very rare occasions they made love.

The only blip in this dry spell was when Rebecca wanted to get pregnant, but then after she gave birth to their daughter, normal service was resumed and months would often go by without any sexual activity at all. Every night they would go to bed in freshly laundered sheets, climbing under their goose-down duvet and… open their books. Rebecca persuaded herself that Frank, like her, wasn't that interested in sex but in reality he was desperately frustrated. He still found Rebecca desirable and wished that that feeling was reciprocated.

At first, Frank secretly watched porn to relieve his frustration, until finally he gave in to temptation. A work colleague started to flirt with him and they began an affair. Rebecca discovered condoms amongst Frank's things, confronted him and he confessed that he couldn't cope with their platonic relationship and had turned elsewhere for sexual fulfilment. Rebecca was distraught that the soulmate she thought she'd be with for life had shattered their relationship for something she considered trivial. Frank was ashamed and upset that he had done this, but knew that he wasn't happy living without sex because it was an important part of who he was.

Although it's tempting to lay the blame at Frank's feet, since he was unfaithful, Rebecca is also part of the problem, because she assumed that Frank was happy with their sexless relationship, rather than addressing it and checking how he felt.

> *If one person wants sex and the other doesn't, there's going to be trouble ahead*

The thread that runs throughout this book, and one that is especially important in this chapter, is firstly knowing what you want and secondly, attracting someone who can give you that. Both Frank and Rebecca should have been clear at the start about their needs – it's all too easy to get wrapped up in the unrealistic 'happily ever after' scenario, but if one person wants sex and the other doesn't, there's going to be trouble ahead.

To return to our house analogy, if our sensual and sexual sides are represented by soft furnishings in our dream homes, how would you feel about living in a stark, minimalist house with white, shiny surfaces? Could you get used to it? Or would you constantly crave an Aladdin's cave of softy, velvety fabrics, filmy curtains and cushions galore? These are metaphors of course, but they can give you an insight into your own persona – what you find attractive and comfortable – and that of any potential partner. Can you see how important it is not only to visualise what you are attracted to but also to find someone who feels the same way?

There is of course the possibility that your initially eppy libido may suffer a slump at some point. When you meet the love of your life (and I'm sure s/he is just around the corner) you won't ever believe that you'll find them anything less than 100% alluring and that just looking at them will send you all a-quiver. But unfortunately, the honeymoon period does end, at approximately the same time that their quirky little habits start to become grating.

According to the NHS website[35], there are lots of reasons why you may experience a loss of libido, the most common one being relationship problems. It makes sense; if you're unhappy with your partner out of the bedroom, you're unlikely to want to leap under the covers with them. There are also health issues such as an underactive thyroid and emotional problems like depression, stress and exhaustion. Our libidos also start to wane as we get older and the menopause can have a big impact. Both men and women have the hormone testosterone, connected with our sex drive, and this starts to dip with age. You also need to consider outside influences, such as hormonal contraception and excessive use of drugs and/or alcohol. If you're struggling with a low libido, ask yourself whether any of the above could be to blame.

SEX AND THE SEXES

Although, as I mentioned at the beginning of the chapter, it's important not to generalise about sexuality, physically, it has been shown that there are some 'male' and 'female' differences around libido and gender. Social psychologist Roy Baumeister[36] reviewed hundreds of different surveys and extrapolated six statistical points, including the interesting nugget that nuns are better at being celibate than priests, with 49% admitting to breaking their rule of chastity compared to 62% of priests (pretty high statistics, I thought!).

1. Men think about sex more often than women

Whilst it's a myth that men think about sex every seven seconds (there is no research that backs up the whopping 8,000 times during waking hours that this would add up to), a study at Ohio State University[37] gave a group of 18-25-year-olds a handheld tally counter and asked them to track whenever they thought about sex, food and sleep. The male participants thought about sex 19 times a day or once every hour and a half, roughly, with food coming in at 18 times and sleep 11 times. The female statistics worked out a sex 10 times a day, food 15 times and sleep 8.5 times. I love the fact that women think about food more times than sex. What about if food and sex were combined, with some chocolate spread sex play? It would be off the scale!

2. Men want more sex than women

"Men want sex more often than women at the start of a relationship, in the middle of it, and after many years of it," says Baumeister. This is the case for all sexualities, gay and straight, although gay men have sex more often than lesbians – and men in general would like more sexual partners and more casual sex than women. Two-thirds of men say they masturbate compared to 40% of women, but women are probably too busy fantasising about food, considering the first sex fact.

3. Women are less straightforward about what arouses them

During a revealing study where devices were attached to participants' genitals (this could have gone very wrong) at Northwestern University in the States, it was found that whilst male physical arousal tallied with what they *said* they were aroused by (male-female sex and female-female sex, or in the case of gay men, male-male sex) straight female arousal was linked to male-female, male-male and female-female, despite the participants saying they were only turned on by male-female sex. So even if women deny having any interest in anything other than heterosexual couplings, the physical evidence says otherwise, which only goes to support what I believe in: the only way to have a satisfying sex life is to be open and honest with yourself – you may surprise yourself with what you discover.

4. Female libido is more affected by social and cultural influences

This idea was backed up by studies in four different areas:
- The way women see sexual acts is more open to change than the way men do
- Women are more affected by what their peer group thinks about sex
- Women who have religious faith are less likely to have permissive attitudes to sex than men
- Women who are more highly educated are said to try a wider range of things in bed, whereas the level of education made no difference in men

The reason why women are more influenced by their environment has a sociological basis: women are left literally holding the baby after sex, so they are more likely to carefully weigh up the benefits of a particular male before having sex, to check that he will make a responsible parent.

5. Female desire originates in the mind

Whilst men view sex as a way of connecting emotionally, women need a more intellectual approach before they feel ready for sex. As New York psychotherapist Esther Perel said: "Women want to talk first, connect first, then have sex. For men, sex *is* the connection. Sex is the language men use to express their tender loving vulnerable side. It is their language of intimacy."

6. Female orgasms are different to male

It's no secret that typically, men climax quicker, on average taking four minutes from penetration to orgasm, whilst women take 10-11 minutes, if they do at all. In a study of couples, 75% of men say they always have an orgasm opposed to 25% of women. There's also a poignant element to this study – whilst the female participants reported the men's rate of orgasm correctly (well, there are some fairly obvious signs…) the men said they believed their female partners climaxed 45% of the time, when in fact it was only 25%. *When Harry Met Sally* has got a lot to answer for.

> *Sex is the language men use to express their tender loving vulnerable side*

Sex is a very complex, primal act, and is much more than just pleasurable. Although casual sex or the 'one-night-stand' is more socially acceptable now than ever before, it still should never be entered into lightly, and should absolutely be consensual for both parties. However, for the couple who have decided to consummate their relationship, having sex steps across an invisible threshold towards a more enduring, longer-term commitment. A new study has found[38] that for both men and women, the more often the couple have sex, the more strongly they associate their partners with positive attributes. This is because we have evolved to choose a mate who we think will provide strong healthy offspring, and even if we don't want children or are using contraception, this is still a subconscious part of our decision-making about a suitable partner. The study found that over time, the amount of sex a couple has is directly related to the couple's attitude towards their relationship. So sex can have a positive effect of reinforcing commitment to the relationship. Also, the more we have sex, the healthier our libido is. It's not the other way around. Our libido is like a muscle, and like all muscles, we need to keep exercising it otherwise we lose it.

So, in a healthy relationship where there is emotional and intellectual compatibility, sex becomes an intimate and connecting experience. But what if this isn't happening? Is this an indication that the relationship isn't really happy? It can be, but it's not necessarily associated with the sex itself. Any number of issues can affect a good love life – from ill health to stress to excess alcohol. So instead of arguing or worrying about the lack of sex and thereby creating even more distance between them, couples need to learn how to really talk and communicate about sex. They also need to be open to hearing what their spouse wants, feels and needs. This is not only a recipe for great sex, but a great marriage as well.[39] It all relates to my fundamental message that communicating our needs is vitally important in every aspect of our lives.

> *The more often a couple has sex, the more strongly they associate their partners with positive attributes*

What's Your Number?

With all these statistics laid bare, it seems that meeting someone who you're totally compatible with under the covers is like finding that proverbial needle in a haystack. If you find yourself in the sticky situation of meeting someone with a higher or lower libido than yourself, don't do a 'Frank and Rebecca' and ignore it, hoping it will go away – instead, acknowledge it and find creative ways around it so that both your wishes are accommodated.

A great article by psychologist Seth Meyers[40] suggests is that you find your 'sex number', that is, to rate how sexual you are between 1 and 10. This helps you navigate the sexual arena much more easily. As a single person, it gives you a good idea of what number you'd like your future partner to be. Alternatively, if you're in a relationship with someone with a lower number than you, knowing it helps you feel less rejected and not take it personally when they're not in the mood very often. A second great idea was to have a menu of sexual acts. That way, it broadens your range of activities and makes it more likely for you to find something you're both willing to do, for example, massage instead of full intercourse. Which brings us back again full circle – being explicit about your needs is the foundation of true sexual happiness.

To help you process all the ideas in this chapter and apply them to yourself, let's take a look at this visualisation exercise. It's a deep subject, so make sure you have a good 15-20 minutes to devote to it without interruption – and use a separate sheet if you need to (I always like clean sheets!).

THE ARCHITECT OF LOVE

1. The root of our *sensual* selves lies in our childhood and what environment we grew up in. What were you surrounded with in your family home? Were there beautiful paintings on the walls and a warm, comforting ambience? Or were the soft furnishings neutral and plain? Did your parents' home feel relaxing to be in, or was it full of pent-up negative energy? Did your parents even bother to make the house a home? Building up an image of what was 'normal' for you in childhood gives you a glimpse of why you're drawn to particular things now.

_____
_____
_____
_____
_____
_____
_____
_____
_____
_____
_____
_____
_____
_____
_____
_____
_____
_____
_____
_____
_____

2. What was your parents' relationship like? Were they tactile with each other in front of you? Did they hug or kiss openly or perhaps it was the opposite, and they were never affectionate and slept in separate rooms? Maybe your parents were separated or divorced and you had a stepfather/mother? Try to think about how this rupture in family life affected you. The answers reveal the building blocks of your own sensuality

_____
_____
_____
_____
_____
_____
_____
_____
_____
_____
_____
_____
_____
_____
_____
_____
_____
_____
_____
_____
_____
_____
_____

3. Now take a moment to visualise your own dream home. What's it like inside? Describe the colours and textures of your soft furnishings in as much detail as possible. Is it similar to your childhood one? History tends to repeat itself unless you consciously want to move away from the lesson learnt in childhood.

KNOWING WHAT YOU WANT

4. How do you feel about your sensual self? Are you happy with your portfolio of experiences or is there a different path you would like to take in future relationships? Visualising your past, present and future will help gauge what direction you would like to take.

5. Do you feel you are truly aware to all the facets of your sexuality? Have you found yourself getting into a rut in the bedroom and do you long to be more experimental? Try to think why this is and imagine the ways this could be realised. What are you attracted to in others? Is sex important in your life? Getting a deeper understanding of how content you are sexually is instrumental in helping you achieve happiness in the future.

CHAPTER FIVE

THE BEDROCK TO HAPPINESS

The Foundation Of Your Home – Your Spirituality

In my childhood growing up in Singapore, the repetitive thud, thud, thud of massive pile-drivers pounding into the earth was a familiar sound. They were laying down the foundations for the office blocks and towers that make up that landscape today. When you look up at the dazzling, mirrored walls of the skyscrapers, soaring up into the clear blue sky, you forget about the enormous amount of steel and concrete buried deep beneath the ground, supporting the structure. Foundations are not glamorous, they're not sexy but they're vital for the survival of the building, helping it withstand all the pressures of every day life.

This is how I see spirituality – as an essential, fundamental and often unseen element of both your emotional make-up and your relationship, supporting you during the stresses and strains life throws at you. In the same way that an anchor steadies a ship during rough seas, hidden deep beneath the water below but providing a crucial role, so spirituality keeps you safe during testing times.

This chapter doesn't have the head-turning wow-factor of the previous chapter's subject, but it is still fundamental to our wellbeing. Before we begin to explore its many facets, I want to address some misconceptions. Many people have an instantaneous negative response to the word 'spirituality'. Either they have a knee-jerk assumption that it's referring to religion, which they may associate with judgment and disapproval, or they are reminded of alternative therapies, crystals and auras. All you atheists out there may be arguing that not believing in God makes it impossible for you to subscribe to spirituality, but even non-believers have a belief system – just like *not* making a decision is still a decision. So spirituality is just that – a belief system, whatever you subscribe to.

An atheist friend of mine says that not having religion is no loss for her, and that the miracle of how the world works – nature, astronomy, even how our own bodies function – is wonder enough and taps into a very spiritual feeling for her. I agree with her and see spirituality as being all around us, infused in everything. It's mind-boggling how human life starts with just a collection of cells, those cells begin to divide, from one to two to four to eight until a fully formed baby arrives, ten fingers and ten toes… It's a miracle. I marvel at these incredible things happening all around us.

So instead of having a narrow-minded view of what spirituality is, I want to blow it wide open so it encompasses everything and anything: a combination of lots of different factors that have influenced your life – lessons you've learnt, your core values, your strengths, your moral compass and your integrity.

If you have a spiritual connection with somebody, it goes beyond chemistry, sexuality or mere attraction – it's almost instinctive. You know how they feel and if they're struggling, you know how to comfort them. It's similar to the bond a mother has with her child. She knows them so intimately that she can predict what they're going to say and how they're going to react, even before they do, sometimes.

The reason why spirituality is so important is like that Bible story about the house built on sand. Everything's hunky-dory until it starts to drizzle and then the inevitable happens, like so many children's sandcastles: 'It fell with a great crash.'[41] If you want a rock-solid relationship, you'd do well to take heed of the core beliefs underpinning it.

The importance of my spiritual connection with my husband came to the forefront 12 years ago when we were hit financially by a business deal. We were cheated out of a large five-figure sum and it had an enormous impact on us. Anders became withdrawn, upset and anxious. He felt that he would be unable to provide for his family. This last factor is such an important element of the male ego – the ability to put food on the table – that when we were threatened in this way, it had huge emotional repercussions.

> *If you want a rock-solid relationship, you'd do well to take heed of the core beliefs underpinning it*

I knew that this was my time to step up to the mark before our family started to crumble. I didn't feel as emotionally blasted by the experience as Anders; I still had the conviction that everything would work out all right in the end, so I worked hard at providing support and reassurance when he was at his lowest ebb. At times I said: "I'm here, how can I help?" at other times, I gave him a pep talk. Gradually, Anders realised that I was there for him, and that come what may, he wasn't on his own having to struggle through it without support – he had me to rely on. I could see what he could achieve in the future and I had unshakeable faith in his abilities and this helped him to recover. What was also crucial during this time was that he understood that he hadn't let us down, and it was this realisation that gave him the strength to pick himself up, dust himself down and continue to be the fantastic professional working man and father that he is.

Without this deep, almost primal link with my husband, it would be all too easy for the relationship to falter. When you're at rock bottom, it can be easy to feel victimised, as if everyone in the world is against you, but if you have an ally who is willing to help you take the first steps to recovery, everything is a lot more bearable. It made me see that together, we are stronger, we give each other the stamina to continue in the most challenging circumstances.

Together Forever

An interesting article that looks closely at spirituality in relationships is on the Psychics Universe website.[42] It suggests that one sign that tells you you're spiritually connected is the feeling that you have known each other forever and that you are comfortable revealing every side of your personality to them. Normally, we have a public persona that we present to the world, showing us in our best light, but with someone you're linked to on a spiritual level, you feel safe enough to reveal 'the real you'. And the wonderful thing about this is that when it happens, it only goes to strengthen the bond you have already formed, as you discover how much you have in common regarding the things that really matter – core values and perspectives on the world.

> *One sign that tells you you're spiritually connected is the feeling that you have known each other forever*

The author of the piece, Mackenzie Wright, goes on to warn that the intensity of a spiritual connection can make it harder to walk away when the relationship becomes dysfunctional. This underlines the point I'm trying to make in this book: that openness and compatibility on so many different levels – intellectual, sexual, spiritual

– is essential for a solid partnership. It's worth trying to ensure that every element of your personality chimes with that of your potential partner before you embark on a relationship.

When I met Anders, as someone with a scientific and mathematical background, he is skeptical about anything spiritual, I was worried that this would be a stumbling block for us. I am open to all kinds of spirituality – not just the Islamic tradition I grew up with, but all world religions, as well as psychics, angels, spirit guides – everything that enables the human race to connect on a deeper level interests me. Unfortunately, this whole realm was a turn-off for Anders. After talking about this deeply on our first dates, we came to the compromise that Anders would learn more about my religious background and I would learn more about his personal belief system. To me it was exciting to delve into each other's psyche in this way, and would be time well spent if we were going to make a commitment to each other. Of course, I wasn't expecting him to convert to my religion, but I was happy that he was making an effort to understand my spiritual make-up and most importantly, keep an open mind about me!

We started off with his preconceptions of what it means to be a Muslim, and I explained my interpretation of it. I then went on to describe how other existential aspects of my nature impacted on my belief system, such as my psychic abilities. He was astonished when I described what had happened when we passed the scene of a recent road accident – the images of what had happened flashed into my mind, and when he googled it, the report confirmed that I was right. Over the course of the next two years, Anders came to understand why my belief system made sense to me.

Gradually, he began to trust that my spiritual abilities were sound, especially after I told Anders that I'd had a bad feeling right from the beginning about the person who defrauded us in the business transaction. After that dreadful experience, his trust in my intuition grew. I instinctively know when to trust someone and what works well for us and our family, because I'm in touch with my spiritual/intuitive side. Similarly, learning about what makes Anders tick on a deeper level and understanding his thought processes and responses to situations has been a great eye-opener for me. I admire his logical approach to life and the way he calmly analyses a given situation or problem, which enables him to come up with the key to resolving it.

The great thing about this spiritual journey we have undertaken together is that Anders has become more in touch with his own spirituality. If we meet a new couple, he is able to intuit how compatible they are. When it comes to our own relationship it gets even better, because since we are spiritually connected, he is able to know instinctively how to soothe me. I have taught him how to speak to my body via massage and if I have a pain somewhere, he knows exactly what to do to ease it. Anders is still the rational science guy with his feet quite firmly on the ground and I still have my head in the clouds sometimes, but instead of this creating friction, it's more harmonious, like yin and yang. We fit together to make a strong unit.

I hope that any sceptics reading this book will, like Anders did, come to realise how crucial spirituality is in our lives. It can be embarrassing to admit to this side of ourselves because to a certain degree it is quite a taboo subject, but if you're open and honest about what it means to you, then you can be sure to find someone who connects with you on the same level. Read Bibi and Henk's story to discover what happens if you don't.

Be True To Yourself

Bibi grew up in Jakarta and was raised as a Muslim. She wasn't particularly strict though and enjoyed a lively social life. Whilst at a nightclub, she met Henk, who was Dutch. They quickly fell in love and set up home together back in Holland. Bibi was head over heels about Henk and because he was not at all religious, she put her own faith to one side. Henk was oblivious to this – to him, Bibi was not a typical Asian woman; she was mixed race, she drank alcohol and she never mentioned Islam. When Henk proposed, Bibi was happy to get married at the City Hall in a civil ceremony – but when Bibi broke the news to her family, they were devastated because she seemed to be turning her back on Islam.

As the years went by, they faced the usual ups and downs – financial worries, redundancies, the arrival of children – and in times of strife Bibi found herself praying to God for guidance. Henk was a deeply secular person and the only seemingly religious ceremony he observed was Christmas, so Bibi kept her reignited faith a secret.

As her children grew up, Bibi felt it important for them to learn about Islam. She knew Henk would disapprove, so she swore them to secrecy. In her heart, she knew this was rather divisive, but she couldn't think of another way of expressing her spirituality to them. But children being children, one day, their secret slipped out and Henk blew up. They had a massive row during which Henk revealed his deep-rooted prejudices against the Islamic culture. Bibi felt both angry and ashamed. She was angry at Henk's reaction and ashamed of secretly doing something he disapproved of.

After much talking, during which tables were banged and tears were shed, Henk and Bibi managed to compromise. Bibi promised to give the children a rounded and realistic view of religion and Henk accepted that Islam was much more than his knee-jerk reaction to it.

It's such a shame that Bibi felt the need to hide that part of her identity. If she had been open from the start telling her husband that she found comfort in prayer, then Henk may have accepted this and grown to love this side of her. It's unrealistic to think that you can ignore someone's heritage because it doesn't sit well with you. To deny someone's past is to deny who they are today. If Henk had been honest with himself and decided that Bibi's faith was a deal breaker for him (which would have been fairly unreasonable, considering they met in Indonesia, a predominantly Muslim country), then the relationship would have ended and they would be free to meet someone more spirituality akin to themselves.

Developing Your Spirituality

In the previous chapters, we've looked at identifying and enhancing the elements that make you shine – making the most of your appearance, becoming more in touch with your emotional intelligence, maximising your brainpower and opening up to your sensuality – but how do you approach spiritual growth? Whilst the other subjects are more readily accessible and relatively easy to incorporate into your lifestyle, how do you make room for spirituality? It would be easy to avoid it altogether by saying you just don't have time to pursue yet another thing in your already crowded schedule, but what if you knew that it would be the secret to a deeper contentment than you've ever known? In a funny way, I already know that you're going to achieve this, because you're reading this book – you've taken a leap of *faith*, and you have a *belief* that there is someone out there for you – so you're already open to spirituality!

It's easier than you think to introduce a sprinkle of spirituality into your life. Try these simple techniques below to get in touch with your spiritual side and if you enjoy them, checkout Anna Borges' article '28 Modern Ways To Become More Spiritual'[43] for further inspiration.

1. Choose a mentor

You may not have a 'spirit guide' but there's no reason why you can't still be motivated and encouraged by someone who you admire. Think of a positive role model – it can be a fictional character, a famous person or even a family member – and tap into their energy. Mine is my late grandmother, who I still feel very much connected to. I have conversations with her in my mind's eye, and feel her guidance in times of trouble. What person do you consider to be wise and intuitive? Is it possible to gain a deeper understanding of life and faith through their good example?

2. Become attuned to colour

It's incredible how uplifting seeing a splash of colour is – a field of sunflowers, a bowl of oranges, the deep blue of the ocean. Bring a little of that magic home by injecting some colour into your wardrobe. Wear red to stay grounded, orange to encourage creativity, yellow and gold for strength, green for personal growth, blue for communication and purple for mysticism.

3. Take note of your dreams

Your dreams are a snapshot of your unconscious mind and it's not often you get such clear picture of what's going on under the surface, so take advantage of this glimpse to help you unravel thorny problems. When interpreting them, trust your instincts instead of seeing the dreams as prophecies. For example, if you dream about a disastrous situation such as a relationship breaking down, it doesn't necessarily mean it's going to happen, just that you may be ready for a new chapter in your life. Dreams are complex and nightmares can be frightening, but in my experience, they do connect with something deeper within us. I have a friend who had recurring dreams about being swamped by a massive tsunami – although she never drowns and can even breathe underwater. On the advice of her therapist, she began to note when she was having the dreams, and how she was feeling. It turned out that the dreams tended to coincide with the times she was feeling overwhelmed with stress. She started to use the dreams as a gauge of her mental health, and began to pre-empt stressful situations by using deep breathing techniques and meditation. Now, she rarely has her tsunami dream.

4. Spread a little love

You're surrounded by people who have made a contribution in your life. Let them know you appreciate it by telling them. Too often we assume our loved ones know they're loved, but actually they may not be feeling appreciated at all. Take the time to make sure they realise how special they are. There is a movement called 'Random Acts of Kindness' where people just do kind things with no expectation of reward – like leaving a casserole on the doorstep of a neighbour who's just had a bereavement, or giving your hat and scarf to a homeless person on the street, or assisting an elderly person with their heavy shopping – except that the rewards, in terms of feeling good about yourself, are massive. Try it sometime.

5. Let go of the grudge
If your blood starts to boil just thinking about someone who's hurt you, it's time to give yourself a break. This doesn't mean accepting the hurt or saying they were right, it just means turning down your emotional thermostat and letting those negative feelings cool a little. Imagine a little room where the cross feelings sit and firmly shut the door on them.

6. Reasons to be cheerful
Ian Dury said it first[44] but a good habit to get into is thinking of three things to be grateful for each day. I do it first thing in the morning, when I wake up, and always with a smile. Don't dwell on the doom and gloom, focus on the good things in life, even if they're just: 'My new socks are really comfortable.' This technique is part of the repertoire of solution-focused hypnotherapy, because actively focusing on positive things in your life starts building those new neural pathways we discussed previously, giving you the opportunity to be expansive and open to new experiences, rather than closed and negative. The smile also makes your brain think you are happy – another tip that can start off your day on a good footing.

7. Connect with the world through nature
Don't go through life on fast forward – press the pause button occasionally to 'stop and smell the roses'. Even if you don't live in a particularly scenic area, there'll still be front gardens to enjoy, a cat licking its paws, the wind rustling the leaves in the trees, the smell of hot buttered toast. What about admiring the red of the sky as you walk home in the evenings? It is important to reconnect with nature because there, more than anywhere, you can experience true peace.

THE BEDROCK TO HAPPINESS

There is a syndrome first defined by Richard Louv[45] called 'Nature Deficit Disorder' which links all sorts of behavioural problems, especially in children, with a lack of connection to the natural world. So, try to use all your five senses to experience everything around you: see the unfurling leaves in spring, hear the birds singing in the trees, touch the cool water of a stream, taste a fresh strawberry off the vine, smell the ozone of the ocean – and reconnect. Using your senses in this way is also a great meditation tool to centre and ground yourself if you're feeling overwhelmed.

8. Choose a mantra

You don't have to be a Hindu or a Buddhist to have a mantra. It can just be a saying that you find uplifting or comforting. I find, "This too shall pass," to be an enormous comfort, especially during particularly trying times with your children or that unreasonable colleague. You could also use, "I am enough," or, "Smile, breathe and go slowly." Pick something that resonates with you.

9. Switch off

Go on a technology fast. Put aside your phone, laptop and tablet and just let yourself 'be' without the distractions of modern life. The other day I was in the supermarket and saw an older lady furiously scrabbling in her handbag, trying to get to her phone before it stopped ringing. She was dropping her money, her groceries and her keys in the process. She managed to find it, but not in time to answer it. She turned to me and said, "I used to manage just fine when I only had a landline," with a rueful smile. There is a phrase 'the tyranny of technology' that sums-up this lady's experience perfectly. We have become slaves to technology rather than its master. A technology fast will allow you to put technology in its rightful place, and will give you more time to truly connect with your friends, your family and your deeper self.

10. Look up

If you're employing the above tip (well done) and are enjoying an evening without TV, why not step outside and enjoy looking at the heavens. Don't worry if you're not an astronomer, simply revel in the wonder of the night sky. Is the moon full? Are there clouds? Can you see any stars? Then just breathe. Whether it makes you ponder the universe or just feel a little shiver about how small we are in comparison, swapping navel-gazing for stargazing really helps put everything into perspective.

See how easy it is to get in touch with your spiritual side? It doesn't demand a huge shift in your thinking, more of a little tweak really. The most helpful tip to get yourself in the right frame of mind is to visualise becoming more open. When I taught belly-dance therapy, I always encouraged my students to stand tall, with their shoulders back so that their heart chakra could shine fully. Try this yourself, and imagine your heart chakra (located around your solar plexus) as a ball of light – both shining out energy and absorbing it. If you're hunched over, you block the ability to make connections with the world around you and to learn and grow from these experiences. Instead of thinking: "I don't like religion," or "I don't agree with that," think: "I wonder why it interests them so much, what has it got to offer?" If you're closed and prejudiced about anything beyond your limited circle of knowledge, then you can never learn anything new and become a better partner/parent/friend.

THE BEDROCK TO HAPPINESS

> *Shine brightly so that your surroundings light up and your partner knows every facet of you*

I like to imagine a truck-driver driving along a dark road. He (or she) needs the headlights on full beam so they can see as far as possible ahead, so they are ready to negotiate the next bend and people can see them coming. It's the same with your relationship to the world and with a partner: shine brightly so that your surroundings light up and your partner knows every facet of you. Read Ann's heart-warming story below to find out how she revealed her own inner light and her unconventional route to a deeper understanding of what spirituality meant to her.

When The Time Is Right

Ann's romantic history was distinctly chequered – she was always in and out of relationships and never really felt she had found 'the one'. She'd had a few longer-term relationships too, but somehow she never quite clicked with them and they broke it off, leaving her heartbroken. She felt that they never really knew or understood the real her. Her Chinese heritage meant that she had been brought up with a belief of karma, but she hadn't paid it much attention.

Ann worked in the entertainment industry, and whilst she was good at her job, she wasn't passionate about it. The endless round of work-related socialising and chatting with superficial people about trivial subjects was starting to make her feel weary. She had always been interested in animal rights and gradually realised that this was her true vocation. She became a vegan and knew that she should leave her job to pursue a life more in keeping with her new beliefs. This was a big decision, so she decided to go to a yoga meditation retreat in Bhutan to make sure she was certain about this life change.

Whilst she was there, she met Peter, who was also exploring his own spiritual path. He was a computer programmer but felt he didn't want to be defined by his job as it wasn't who he truly was. When Ann and Peter talked, it was like the last piece of a puzzle finally slotting into place. They both knew that while neither was perfect, they were perfect for each other. They recognised in each other something no one else had – a deep spiritual connection that was nourishing and fulfilling. In the remote retreat in Bhutan, they both felt like they were coming home. Was this a bit of good karma coming Ann's way? Their relationship quickly flourished and they were ready to start their new lives together, fortified by their shared values.

It's only when Ann was true to herself and what she really wanted in life, that she was able to find peace. The first part of her life was spent in the pursuit of what she thought made her happy, but ultimately her destiny lay elsewhere. Luckily she had the courage to venture out of her comfort zone and explore what else the world had in store for her.

How Can You Encourage Spirituality In A Relationship?

If your primary goal is to find your soulmate, you may not consider finding ways to become more spiritual as a couple to be a priority, thinking: "Well, I need to get a date first!" but just like those foundations in a house, spirituality is an unseen but essential part of someone's makeup, and having it on your radar whilst you're out looking is important. In an interesting article H. Norman Wright[46] writes about how one woman previously described her relationship as 'ho-hum' until her husband admitted that he prayed for her every day. She felt a sudden rush of love for him and a closeness that she had never felt before. The courage it took him to reveal this secret was rewarded many times over with a greater intimacy and togetherness never experienced before.

The spiritual connection I have with my husband helps me accept the different twists and turns we face on our journey together. As we are both global nomads, sharing similarly restless souls, I can recognise the signs when he's ready for a new adventure, a new project, or a new country to explore. Because we have this common bond, I am prepared for when he announces its time to move on, and I will have researched it, looking at where we would be happy and how we could go about it. I accept that that is part of who he is and I know I need to be positive for him and for ourselves.

Do you wonder how can you encourage this intimacy in your own relationships in the future? To be in the right frame of mind when you meet your new soulmate, bear these ideas in mind:

Have double vision

For a true spiritual partnership, you need to be supportive and understanding of each other's deepest desires. Make sure you know what your partner's dreams are and help towards the fulfilment of them. Equally, don't be afraid to share your own hopes for the future. If these two don't immediately appear to gel, then think creatively to compromise.

Be your best self

If you enter into a relationship with the clear intention of always moving forward, growing and evolving into the person you aspire to be, then your partner will naturally support you and endeavour to do the same themselves. For example, if your goals are lowly, such as aiming to cover the bills and mortgage each month, then that's where you'll stay, but if you aim higher, challenging yourself with new experiences, then the relationship will flourish into something exciting and full of potential.

Examine your exes

It's no good thinking: "The next relationship is the one that is going to make me happy," you have to make peace with the old ones first. It's tempting to wonder what you were thinking of when you review your 'ex portfolio' but there was a reason at the time that made him or her attractive to you, and it's important to respect that. If it was your partner who ended the relationship, let go of the hurt – you wouldn't want to be with someone who doesn't want to be with you, now would you? And if you were the one to call it a day, remember what initially attracted you to them in the first place. Look at what the attractions were; look at what the problems were; see if there are any patterns that you can learn from – then move on, ensuring that you don't make the same mistake twice.

Go with the flow
Understand that to grow as a person involves accepting change. This is a core belief of Buddhist philosophy – in the circle of life we are in an endless process of life, death and rebirth, ever fluctuating. Equally, your relationship won't stay preserved in aspic – it too will evolve. This reminds me of someone I met whose love of their life died. He was truly her soulmate and she never believed she would find anyone else again. He died when their children were young and she had to raise them on her own, giving her huge stamina and resilience. Years later she went on to find happiness in another relationship – this time with a real go-getting businessman, someone she previously wouldn't have been attracted to. She realised that this was because her life experiences had changed her so that he was now the right person for her and vice versa. Change was essential for her to find a second soulmate.

Remember the power of touch
Physical contact is so healing and comforting. It's not an urban myth that giving a child's hurt knee a kiss really does 'make it better', as it helps the child release feel-good endorphins. Touch is an invaluable way of staying

connected with your partner so don't shy away from a goodbye hug or a chance to snuggle on the sofa.

Ask for the moon
A central theme in this book is visualisation, particularly visualising how you would like your ideal partner to be. Here, it's especially pertinent. Itemise the dream qualities your partner has, then adopt them yourself. For example, if a GSOH (good sense of humour) is a must, make the most of your funny bone yourself. Just as Gandhi said, "Be the change you want to see in the world," I say, "Become the person you want to meet," because like attracts like, and so you're sure to attract someone because they recognise and approve of the mirrored version of themselves.

Give them a daily boost
If you want your partner to be the most special person on the planet for you, then you have to treat them as if they are. After you've had that thrilling first date, try to make a note of how you felt so you can recreate the magic again and again. It's these experiences that make us feel good, both about ourselves and each other. When the relationship becomes established, don't let things slide, continue to make a fuss of them, cook their favourite meals, complement them regularly and notice the little things they've done. Act as if they're the best thing since sliced bread and they will be!

> *Act as if they're the best thing since sliced bread and they will be!*

Be ready to flex with the stresses
To return to the analogy of a house, the time when it's most vulnerable is when it's threatened by outside forces,

such as a hurricane or earthquake, and this is why strong foundations are absolutely essential. Lateral-thinking architects all around the world are creating new ways to cope with such attacks, such as bouncy rubber layers in the foundations, shock absorbers placed at regular intervals between the floors of the buildings and even a cushion of air that inflates under the building at the first tremor, just like a car's airbag. In the same way, add flexibility to your armoury. Be prepared to adapt to survive. Here's how Esther and Kevin found new ways of coping when they faced one of life's biggest challenges.

THE BEDROCK TO HAPPINESS

Spiritual Strength

Esther and Kevin were a happy match. They were both raised as Christians and met during a church gathering. Spirituality was important to them as individuals and also as a couple. It provided an incredibly strong foundation for their relationship, and sharing the same values meant that theirs was a generally harmonious household. The crunch came when Kevin had a diagnosis of cancer, but instead of testing their faith, they discovered that it provided not only emotional strength but practical support too. During Kevin's gruelling treatment, they would go to the hospital chapel to pray together and they truly believed that they could fight the demon of cancer armed with their faith.

Unfortunately, Kevin's health deteriorated and he had to have further, more specialised treatment. Since they were in the US, they were reliant on their health insurance, and this new medical procedure wasn't covered. They were forced to sell their home to pay the medical bills and downsize to a smaller apartment. Esther also had to find a job when Kevin became too ill to work.

As well as their faith giving them the stamina to carry on, it also helped massively in practical terms, as their local church community rallied around, providing childcare for them when Kevin had hospital appointments and raising funds for them when they were in dire financial straits.

This network of loving care – each other, God and their family and friends – carried Kevin and Esther through the hardest times in their lives and made them even more certain of the importance of having a faith. Without this support, they felt they would surely have crumbled. Happily, Kevin went on to make a full recovery, and he now is able to give back to his community the love and support he received during his illness.

As well as the traditional view of spirituality – belief in God – they also found strength in their mutual spiritual connection and that of their community's too. This poem below by Khalil Gibran[47] encapsulates everything I believe about the perfect relationship, and it is expressed so wonderfully too.

On Marriage

You were born together, and together you shall be forevermore.
You shall be together when the white wings of death scatter your days.
Ay, you shall be together even in the silent memory of God.
But let there be spaces in your togetherness.
And let the winds of the heavens dance between you.
Love one another, but make not a bond of love.
Let it rather be a moving sea between the shores of your souls.
Fill each other's cup, but drink not from one cup.
Give one another of your bread, but eat not from the same loaf.
Sing and dance together and be joyous, but let each one of you be alone.
Even as the strings of a lute are alone though they quiver with the same music.
Give your hearts, but not into each other's keeping.
For only the hand of life can contain your hearts.
And stand together, yet not too near together.
For the pillars of the temple stand apart.
And the oak tree and the cypress grow not in each other's shadow.

Such a beautiful, inspiring poem should leave you in the perfect mood for contemplating the visualisation exercise below. This time, we're looking at your own spiritual foundations and those of your future partner. Think deeply about your response.

THE BEDROCK TO HAPPINESS

1. Thinking back to your childhood home, how safe did you feel in your family? Did you feel like everything could collapse at any moment, or did you feel pretty secure? When your parents argued, did you ever feel like it was your fault or did you know it had nothing to do with you and their love for you?

2. Do you feel your childhood years provided you with a good basis for you to grow into a spiritually mature person? If not, what can help you now to grow into the best version of you?

3. Now take another deep breath, clear your mind of the past and let's think of the future. When you imagine your future home, what is it like structurally? What materials are attractive to you, for example, steel, wood, stone, brick. Look at the qualities and strengths of these materials. How do they correlate with the characteristics of your ideal partner?

4. Imagine your home being battered by a strong typhoon or gale-force winds. It would only be sustained by strong foundations – just like a good relationship. If a future relationship faced stormy weather, what would you do to shore it up and ensure that it survived the tumult?

_____
_____
_____
_____
_____
_____
_____
_____
_____
_____
_____
_____
_____
_____
_____
_____
_____
_____
_____
_____
_____
_____
_____
_____
_____

5. Now think about the kind of partner you want to have. What kind of spiritual connection would you like? What would your shared values be? How would you envisage tackling the inevitable hardships that come your way?

CHAPTER SIX

EVERYTHING IN THE GARDEN IS ROSY

Your Location – The People Around You

You have your beautiful house but your work is by no means over. Now is the time to look at its surroundings. Remember the estate agent's maxim – the three most important things to consider when buying a house: location, location, location? It's not enough to have your dream home, whether it's a canal boat with a painted bucket of flowers on the roof or a modernist concrete block with steel girders in pride of place, you've got to make sure it's in a pleasing setting too. That canal boat doesn't want to be moored under a flyover, in a stagnant pool of water with discarded shopping trolleys on the towpath, and the modernist apartment would look much better situated on a chic, waterside wharf than in an industrial estate behind a supermarket.

It's true to say that the impact of your environment on your ideal home is massive. Opening your curtains and surveying your outside space can either lift or dampen your mood. Imagine how you'd feel if the view from your bedroom window was a beautifully tended garden with a flourishing vegetable patch, immaculate lawn and flower beds in full bloom. Your spirits would lift a little every day just seeing it. Now imagine that the garden was more of a scrapyard, with piles of old junk, car tyres, empty bottles and broken glass. You'd feel like shutting the curtains again and getting straight back into bed. What you choose to surround your home with is a real reflection of your personal wellbeing and the impression you give to the world.

To continue our house analogy, I see where your home is located as being equivalent to the people you are surrounded by. To create a comfortable environment where you are happy and ready to meet a new soulmate, you have to look at what outside influences are affecting you and actively work at creating the best setting for yourself. In practical terms, this means taking a look at who is in your social circle and deciding whether they contribute to or jeopardise your overall happiness.

> *You are the average of the five people you spend the most time with*

You are much more likely to make the right life choices if you are surrounded by people whose opinions and lifestyles you respect and admire. When my husband and I lived in the Netherlands we got to know a young Irish colleague of Anders'. He had gravitated towards my husband because he was in awe of his professional ability. He would come and spend time with us because he enjoyed our relaxed weekend lifestyle: long, leisurely meals, conversations and lots of laughs reminded him of 'having a craic' back home in Ireland. I think he became a little infatuated with me, too, and generally wanted to emulate what Anders had – a successful career and a happy relationship. A few years later, we caught up with him again and he was happily married to his own Asian wife and they were living the kind of life he'd been envisioning. I wonder where he'd be now if he had chosen to hang around with his peers? Still single, I imagine, and yearning for a lifestyle that seemed out of his reach.

World-renowned motivational speaker Jim Rohn once said: "You are the average of the five people you spend the most time with,"[48] and he's right, we are affected by who we socialise with. Take a look at your social circle – does it include mood-hoovers and emotional vampires? Are there people who you spend time with out of duty or a sense of pity? Is the friendship mutually beneficial or is it more of a one-way street?

Try this exercise to find out who's influencing you.

1. Get a piece of paper and write down how you spend your day, divided into categories for work, home life and socialising. Take a look at the major players in those different spheres – your work colleagues, your relatives and friends.
2. Next, pick from this list the five people who you spend the most time with and go through them one by one, asking yourself: who is this person? What is their outlook on life? Are they moving forward or are they stuck in a rut? Do they constantly complain about their life or do they do something about the things that make them unhappy? Do they come up with new projects or do they shy away from challenges?
3. Now ask yourself what their relationship is to you. Are you forever buoying them up, or do they help you too? Do you tend to provide the role of 'parent' or do you have equal status? With regards to colleagues, do they respect your work and encourage you, or do they squash and undermine your efforts?
4. Ask yourself how these relationships have affected you in the long-term. Perhaps you used to suggest interesting activities but have stopped bothering after one too many negative reactions? Or maybe you once came up with creative solutions to work problems but these were brushed aside. If you constantly receive negative feedback, two things

happen. Firstly, you stop trying to impress the people around you and secondly, you start to believe their downbeat thinking, and even echo it yourself, peppering your speech with phrases such as: "What's the point?" and, "Just do the bare minimum."
5. Finally, ask yourself if you want to change who you spend time with. Choose people who lighten the load rather than add to your burden. Set yourself a goal of achieving something – whether it's to get a promotion, find a new partner or moving house – and then carefully select the people on your list who would enhance your chances of success, either by pushing you forward or by simply being the sort of person you aspire to be.

This may seem a little self-serving, and you may think, "I can't abandon my friend just because she's grumpy and never listens to me," but that's not what I'm suggesting: I'm not saying to never speak to them again, I'm simply suggesting that you align yourself with people who you feel will help motivate and challenge you to be the best you possibly can me. Your old friends will stay friends, but perhaps you don't see them quite as much as you used to.

We're social animals, we live in tribes and need others to make us feel good. It can feel incredibly harsh to simply slough-off people who don't fulfil a role in our lives, but ultimately, why are you spending precious time being with them if they are dragging you down? Read James' story for a glimpse of what can happen if you don't shake up your lifestyle when it's no longer where you want to be.

Peter Pan Faces Reality

For the whole of his adult life, James has done exactly what he wanted. He works hard, earns a six-figure salary in corporate banking and enjoys letting his hair down the rest of the time – going to nightclubs, in the VIP box at football matches, dining in fancy restaurants. James is good-looking, takes care of himself and never troubles himself with worries about time passing. Despite being in his forties, he's still living the life of a twenty-something. The only negative part of this rosy scene is James' love life. It's a conundrum. On the one hand, he is attracted to younger women because he likes to 'rescue' them and take care of them, tending to pick very glamorous but quite immature women. On the other hand, he wonders if his choice of girlfriend is really making him happy. Are these women genuinely interested in him or are they 'gold-diggers,' just after him for a share in his lavish lifestyle? He doesn't have much of a connection with them and feels unable to develop anything more than a superficial relationship where he becomes the sugar daddy.

His group of friends don't help. They're misogynistic and have a warped view of relationships. They treat the women they date appallingly, they pick them up and drop them without a second thought and often string two or three along at once. The laddish culture that they exist in condones this and they don't think to question the morality of it.

The one exception to the rule is James' friend Andrew. Andrew met and fell in love with his intellectual match over 15 years ago – an intelligent woman who has a career of her own. James envies Andrew's relationship and wishes he could settle down too. He has never found 'the one' and wonders whether he ever will. As the years go by and he watches Andrew's relationship thrive and grow whilst he continues to be a serial dater, he asks himself where he went wrong.

James had a glimpse of a life path that he could have taken, with his friend Andrew, but for some reason he chose to remain in a lifestyle more appropriate to a much younger man. He claims he could never find 'the one' but it's highly unlikely that he ever will if he only hangs out with that social circle – 'lads' and young, impressionable women. What worked for him in his twenties has stopped working now and the reason is because he is resisting change and stopping his life from moving forwards and evolving. If you recognise elements of yourself in James, find out how you can start to extricate yourself from a social circle that has stopped being helpful.

How To Stop Seeing Toxic Friends

I've always liked the saying: 'Friends for a reason, friends for a season and friends for life.' It emphasises the fact that people come and go throughout your life – one moment you're best mates, the next you've drifted apart and the intensity of the first few weeks has died away. We're conditioned to feel that friendship is permanent and we must remain loyal, come what may. But this type of thinking is not always helpful. Needing people around us is a primal instinct, dating back to when we were cavepeople, fighting off threats from wild animals. There is safety in numbers, it's true, but in the 21st century sabre-tooth tigers are less of a worry and we can pick and choose who we socialise with.

Friendships can develop for lots of different reasons: some are due to proximity, such as a neighbour, a work colleague or the person on the next mat to you at yoga class, or due to a shared interest, like football or reading. Others have begun because the friend is also going through a specific phase in their life as you are, such as having young children or going to college. It's comforting and positive to have fellow travellers on the journey of life who you can swap stories with and offer advice to but sometimes you need to stop and ask yourself whether they're a hindrance more than a help. According to www.2knowmyself.com[49], friends can change your beliefs, affect your self-confidence, affect your behaviour and influence your mood. That's quite a lot of power in their hands, so it makes sense to be sure they're a force for good. Try these tips to extricate yourself when you realise your friend is actually more of a 'frenemy'.

Trust your instincts
Look at your diary of upcoming events and ask yourself: "Do I really want to meet up with her/him?" Are you just doing it out of habit when actually seeing that person is not much fun, and hasn't been for some time? "Sometimes the earliest sign is that you leave outings with that person feeling drained, rather than energised," says Andrea Bonior Ph.D., author of The Friendship Fix[50]. "Often, you notice that when you're with this person, you are not your best self in interacting with them. Perhaps you tend to be more snarky, passive-aggressive, judgmental or competitive. Or you notice that you don't really want the best for that person." This is a clear sign that you're not benefiting from the friendship and should withdraw from it.

Tweak the connection
If you value a friendship but there are isolated areas that bother you, try broaching these issues with the person. For example, if someone is generally supportive, but always makes a point of criticising your partner, then address it

with them. They may not be aware that they're doing it or they may not have realised that it upsets you. (It may be that since you moan about him/her they assumed that they could just join in, breaking the unwritten rule that it's okay for *you* to pick faults with your partner but no one else!) You don't have to have a serious talk, just gently comment: "Hey, that's a bit unfair," when they overstep the mark and hurt your feelings.

Be firm but compassionate
If you've definitely recognised that you no longer want to be friends, make it clear in a way that isn't devastating for them. Hurling insults is not the solution. Instead, try saying something that acknowledges your part in the relationship and doesn't apportion blame, such as: "I'm finding these chats hard, I'd like to take a break from them." They will go away feeling that it's your problem, not theirs. You never know, it may even make them examine their behaviour and address what made them toxic to you, or even if they just think, "Your loss," it's much kinder and leaves you in a much better space, emotionally. You were honest but not hurtful. As for the way you do it, I'd recommend via the phone rather than face to face. It gives them time to process their emotions by themselves. Definitely never via a text – it's too dismissive and easily can be misinterpreted.

Enlighten them
However, if you genuinely feel they would benefit from knowing why you're breaking contact, then tell them. Perhaps they're oblivious to their continual put-downs and negativity, in which case you could point it out, framing it in a constructive way, such as: "I find that always imagining the worst-case scenario is counter-productive, it doesn't

really help anyone. Have you thought about trying to look on the bright side?" They may be offended but if they are, then I bet they're the type to take offence at everything anyway. Another reason why you don't need them around.

Keep schtum
When you decide to part ways with a friend, be discreet about it. Don't mention it to anyone else in your social circle. There are three good reasons for this. Firstly, it's much more sensitive to keep your reasons to yourself – the ex-friend could easily find out from a 'helpful' third party and would probably hear your words phrased in a much less favourable way. Secondly, announcing to all and sundry that you're 'chucking' your friend is quite alarming and will cause shock waves throughout your social circle. It will cause them to question your loyalty and cast doubt on their allegiance to you. Keep it a private matter between the two of you to minimise speculation amongst the rest of the crowd. The third reason is that complaining about a friend is just perpetuating the negative energy that already existed around this friendship. Make a clean break and put it behind you, leaving the future clear for more productive friendships.

To return to the garden analogy, a toxic friend could be likened to an old tree that stopped being beautiful years ago, that no longer blossoms or bears fruit, and has grown twisted and gnarled. You've tolerated it for ages even though it casts a shadow over your lawn, and its roots are growing into your foundations, causing damage. You hesitate to chop it down because you used to be fond of it – but actually, leaving it there is doing more harm than good. In the same way, you don't need a friend who overshadows you and makes you feel unhappy – don't put up with them just because you feel you should. Instead, cultivate (a nod to the garden analogy!) new friends who want the best for you and always have your best interests at heart. As Deepak Chopra says, "Negative people deplete your energy. Surround yourself with nourishment and do not allow the creation of negativity in your environment."[51]

A fascinating article on the website www.statesmanshs.org[52] looks at how the interplay of friends, peers and that other crucial influence in our lives, our family, all work towards moulding our personalities. In it, psychologist Stacey Max suggests that you're born with a certain temperament, for example, you can be an introvert even though you belong to a family of extroverts, and then the people and experiences around you shape you. So it's a combination of nature and nurture that makes us who we are. The article goes on to describe how our parents are the first socialising agents that we know and then, when we become more independent, we become open to outside influences, such as schoolmates, teachers and activity leaders.

The interesting point is that our temperaments continue to have a say in this interaction. When you find yourself gravitating towards a certain person or group, and you feel that they really chime with your values and expectations in life, it's most likely to be because your personality matches with those in the group. If there is a personality clash, then you are more likely to put up barriers and reject what the group has to offer, regardless of the content.

This just shows that our influences are fluid and a two-way street. We gain from being around like-minded people and we are more likely to buy into what they have to say and contribute towards the group if we feel comfortable around them.

During adolescence, we naturally move away from our parents and start to develop our own identities, drawing on what we see around us to form our perspective on the world. Reassuringly for those parents out there, the values that have been instilled in the child's early years stay with them when they are making choices about who to befriend.

Childhood is such a critical time for building self-esteem, confidence and stability that it's harrowing what happens if the child's emotional development is disturbed by neglect or abuse. Read Rahayu's story for an example of the resilience of the human spirit and the damage that can be done when those around you let you down.

From Darkness to Light

Rahayu is a dynamic, grounded and open woman who has dedicated her life to helping others. She lives in Malaysia and has set up a support centre for women with HIV – a much-needed resource as there is still a lot of ignorance and prejudice around this disease there. She does all she can to help these women and educate the wider community about how HIV is actually spread, to help eradicate the scaremongering that exists currently. Her life is full of positivity and growth. Sadly, it wasn't always this way.

She came from an extremely abusive marriage, where her husband sold her to a brothel after the birth of their fourth child. He had run up massive debts due to a heroin addiction and even sold off the birth certificates and passports of his wife and children to pay off debts. Sadly, she contracted HIV from him and it seemed like her situation couldn't get any worse. She spent her life living in fear, avoiding eye contact on the street in case anyone noticed she was a street worker, as in Malaysia that meant being sent to a draconian prison. All she could think off was feeding her four kids who were all homeless and living under a bridge.

One day, head down and scurrying along, she literally bumped into someone. She recoiled in fear then looked up to see a friendly, smiling face. "Don't be afraid," the man said. "I know exactly how you feel, because I was once there too. Let me help you." As Rahayu looked into his eyes, she felt all her worries fade away. The man, Rosli, turned out to be Rahayu's guardian angel. He was true to his word and over the following months, he helped her to leave the brothel and start her emotional and physical rehabilitation.

When Rahayu asked why he was doing this, he explained that he too had followed the same painful path as her husband – drugs, HIV, prison. He knew what life was like on the streets. A street pastor had helped him get back on track, and he decided to do the same, to 'pay it forward'. Rahayu and Rosli fell in love and are now happily married, both working to help others who faced the troubles they did.

Rahayu's youthful years with her first husband were such an ordeal, yet it is heartening to see that despite such trauma, she was still able to be open to the positive influence of Rosli, who showed her that recovery and even happiness was possible. Rahayu's story also proves that shared experiences count for a lot – she was receptive to Rosli's advice because she recognised in him her own pain – he had experienced similar difficulties and so truly understood how she felt. The cherry on the cake is that not content with improving her own wellbeing, she is now sharing what she has learnt with fellow HIV sufferers and helping them to cope with the condition, thus having a positive influence on others.

The fact that our environment has such an impact on our life decisions, particularly dangerous ones like drug use, is never clearer than with the famous 'Rat Park' experiment by Professor Bruce Alexander of Vancouver University.[53] Back in the 1970s, he set up an experiment using two rats in two cages. One cage was empty and the other was full of rat-friendly objects and activities to keep its occupant happy. Both rats were given two bottles of water, one was uncontaminated, the other laced with morphine and the rats could decide which bottle to drink from. Both rats sampled both types of water in their water-feeders but the big difference is that the rat that was forced to endure a miserable existence in a bare cage became addicted to the morphine-water whilst the rat that had plenty to occupy itself chose to drink the pure water.

Professor Alexander concluded that this reframed the reasons for drug-use completely. Rather than it being a sign of weakness or because your brain becomes dependent on the chemical, it's an 'adaptation', or a change in your behaviour to cope with your environment. In our garden analogy, if every time we step outside we tread on broken glass, we numb the pain with painkillers – why wouldn't we?

If you're sceptical as to whether a rat's decision-making can really translate into the human experience, the results of this experiment have also been documented in real people, specifically soldiers in the Vietnam War. As addiction expert and author Johann Hari commented in his article in The Huffington Post[54], heroin use in US soldiers was, "as common as chewing gum" and 20% of users became addicted. The surprising thing was that when the soldiers returned home, they stopped taking heroin completely, often without any rehab. Their nightmare environment had returned to a pleasurable one so they no longer needed to escape from it. This means that instead of blithely going through life oblivious to what's going on around you, it makes sense to stop and examine what factors there could be that are subconsciously affecting you (and remember, your emotional wellbeing is essential if you want to find a partner, as we discussed in Chapter Two).

Virtual Isolation

Day-to-day encounters with people are the obvious starting point, but don't overlook something as seemingly innocuous as going online. We're increasingly turning to the internet for social interaction in chat rooms, forums, social media networks and more. The good thing is that it's enabled us to be in touch with people all around the world and is in some ways a great social leveller – anyone and everyone can have a Twitter account or a Facebook page. One of the downsides, however, is that whilst we're sat in front of a laptop, chatting online, we're actually isolating ourselves from genuine, meaningful relationships IRL (in real life, to use digital slang). It's easy to interpret the cosy banter on a forum as true intimacy but how often have you heard about (or experienced) the disappointment of a really promising email exchange via online dating, only to discover when you meet up that there is absolutely no spark? Digital connections are no substitute to proper, face-to-face meetings.

It reminds me of that addictive computer game FarmVille. You devote hours and hours to cultivate a beautiful virtual farm and when you look up from your computer you discover that your real-life garden is withering from neglect – how ironic!

> *Digital connections are no substitute to proper, face-to-face meetings.*

You would think that your email pinging all day with social network updates would inevitably keep your mood buoyant, but John Cacioppo of the University of Chicago[55] has discovered that it's very much dependent on who those pings are from. Just as we're influenced by people's moods around us in the real world, so we are in our online community. His research has revealed that if a close connection (or 'friend' in Facebook terms) is lonely, you are 52% more likely to be lonely yourself. This is because loneliness exhibits itself in certain unfriendly behaviours that we end up mimicking. So if your lonely friend posts grumpy, negative, self-pitying or defensive comments, you are influenced by this and start to behave that way too to others, thus perpetuating the vicious circle. This suggests that you are vigilant when chatting to online friends as you are with 'real' friends, and remember that their moods are not only infectious but also just a click away.

Loneliness is very much a buzzword in psychological circles at the moment but instead of fearing it, we should see it as an early-warning sign that something is wrong. In Oliver Burkeman's always enlightening column in *The Guardian* newspaper[56], he actually sees loneliness as a good thing. This is because this emotion is a symptom that we shouldn't ignore. If you're on our own and perfectly content, then everything's hunky dory, but if you've been by yourself for too long and are feeling unhappy, then it motivates you to do something about it. Also, loneliness actually makes us value our friends and family more when we reconnect with them.

It's hard when we feel isolated in the midst of our community but sadly it happens more often than we'd like. One reason can be cultural differences, meaning that our values don't chime with those around us. One person that springs to mind is Amr, someone I met in Egypt. He was happily married to his wife and had chosen to remain monogamous, rather than have several wives, as was the custom in his community. He was ridiculed for this, and also for his decision to help his wife with housework and childcare. Luckily, he felt strong enough to tolerate the unpleasant comments, mainly because he was supported by his parents, who were the reason he held these views. Another huge boost was that he worked for a German company, so many of his colleagues had similar 'Western' views as him. Just because you're born into a certain culture, doesn't mean that you have to adopt its ways. This can create friction, but so long as you have your own tribe within that culture, you can still feel secure.

This resonates strongly with my own personal experience as a global nomad. Since I have lived in many different cultures, I have learnt how to adapt so I fit right in, whilst still keeping my own beliefs. This is why I call my company Seventh Tribe, because these are people who are rootless and can adopt any community as their own.

Having faith in your own convictions despite outside influences requires strength and determination. Sometimes you need to be a little creative to maintain high spirits when negative vibes are fizzing. I have a friend who used to work in an office with a very unpleasant boss, who would bully, belittle and victimise his employees. They all used to socialise on Fridays after work and inevitably, the conversation would turn to his latest misdemeanour, and the topic would stay firmly on that for the rest of the evening. This monstrous employer was pervading their social lives even when they weren't at work. They realised that to properly enjoy their leisure time, they'd have to leave all 'shop talk' including any mention of the boss at the office, and a swear box was introduced, fining anyone who mentioned his name.

> *Do whatever it takes to protect yourself from damaging influences*

Drastic measures, it may seem, but you need to do whatever it takes to protect yourself from damaging influences. They didn't want to leave a good job, so instead they found a way of holding the bully at arms' length. Carefully compartmentalising your day so you keep your 'work head' firmly in the office is a good strategy for managing stressful conditions, but sometimes it's not possible to prevent negative influences if they dominate your life. Maria's story is a good illustration of when enough is enough.

A Marriage of Convenience?

When Maria met Sebastian they were both in their early twenties and he was her first serious boyfriend. She was instantly attracted to his charisma and intelligence. He had been a child prodigy and now grown, was able to talk about any subject at length, with great knowledge and insight. His intellect knew no bounds and he was a fascinating person to be with. Maria fell deeply in love. The couple went to visit Sebastian's parents and they gave her a very warm welcome. She felt privileged to be made part of the family.

However, Maria discovered that Sebastian's brilliance came at a price – he also suffered from terrible mood swings, where he would sink into deep depressions, fly into rages over nothing and develop delusions of grandeur. Unsure as to how to help him, she contacted his parents, who, instead of being concerned, were unsurprised about Sebastian's mental health; he had a long history of breakdowns and they were just glad that he had found someone willing to put up with him. Instead of sympathy, they threw money at the problem, paying for Sebastian's treatment in private retreats and giving Maria a generous income to live on.

Because Maria was young and impressionable, she decided she loved Sebastian so much that she was willing to support him and they went on to marry and have children. Sadly, after several years, Sebastian's mental health problems grew intolerable. He became very controlling and critical and Maria didn't recognise this unpleasant, narcissistic bully.

He wasn't the man she married. She tried to explain the situation to her parents-in-law but they refused to discuss it. Their main concern was that she provided a stable base for Sebastian and looked after their grandchildren – her own emotional needs were ignored.

Finally, Maria realised that she had to leave Sebastian for the sake of her sanity and for her children's wellbeing too. His family immediately stopped all financial support and launched a complicated legal case to ensure she would never receive a penny of alimony. Despite this cruelty, Maria felt nothing but relief to be out of this toxic situation. Sebastian and his parents never had any direct contact with her again and for this, she was glad.

I'm sure we can empathise with Maria's difficult decision – it's easy to hope that love will conquer all and that the positive aspects of a relationship will smooth over any problems. But this is not often the case – love can turn to hate if a toxic situation cannot be resolved. But as Maria bravely acknowledged, Sebastian's behaviour was too much to bear and the initial poverty and loneliness was a price she was prepared to pay to alleviate the fear and sadness she experienced with the marriage. We should take Maria's story as an example, and take a long, hard look at the people we surround ourselves with: what we can tolerate, what we can improve and what we must rid ourselves of to make sure that, 'everything in the garden is rosy'.

It's time to contemplate your own vision of your perfect surroundings in order to achieve the most fulfilling social circle you can have. This in turn will enable you to move towards the ideal relationship, so close your eyes, take a deep breath, relax your mind and we'll go back in time.

THE ARCHITECT OF LOVE

1. Think back to your childhood home – was it one where family and friends were welcomed, or were you quite an insular family with few external connections? Is there any particular person that stands out from that period? How did this person make you feel?

EVERYTHING IN THE GARDEN IS ROSY

2. Now think about whether anyone had an impact on your family life – did you have endearing grandparents who helped your parents to cope? Were you friendly or frosty with your neighbours? How might these childhood relationships be relevant to your current ones?

3. Now close your eyes again, clear your mind of the past, take another deep breath and visualise all the faces of the close friends and family today who you spend a lot of time with. Why do you choose to spend time with these individuals? Pick at least one person whose relationship you admire. What is it about it that impresses you? If there isn't one, ask yourself, "Have I purposely been avoiding contact with people who have happy relationships?"

EVERYTHING IN THE GARDEN IS ROSY

4. Imagine you are the garden designer in your future home: what will it be like? Tropical, manicured or rambling? Now imagine a particular element of your outside space, such as a beautiful flower or a shady veranda, and try to visualise the person that element represents. This is someone who you perceive to be a positive influence on you and your relationships.

THE ARCHITECT OF LOVE

5. If you could choose three inspiring people to be at your garden party, who would they be and why?

EVERYTHING IN THE GARDEN IS ROSY

6. Since this is your last visualisation exercise I would now like you to take stock of the whole house and garden that you have visualised during the exercises in this book. What does it look like? Describe your ideal home in detail, and then relate it to your ideal partner. Take your time – this is important. Remember that you are the architect, you hold the pen to redraw the plans if need be. Is there anything else about this whole house (from Chapter 1 to here) that needs changing or addressing?

CHAPTER 7

ROAD BLOCKS & SPEED BUMPS

Obstacles To Overcome

You are now fully equipped to embark on the greatest adventure of your life: finding your soulmate, that perfect person to love, who will love you in return. But before you embark on such a big project, it's always good to prepare yourself for any obstacles that may stand between you and happiness. I liken these to road-blocks, because they hinder your progress towards your dream. These obstacles can take many different forms including people, beliefs and lifestyle choices, and you need to be heedful of these negative influences around you, so you can sidestep them. Sometimes you may not even be aware that they are obstructing you – it's only when you take a moment to reflect that you realise that a person's behaviour, and also more importantly, how they make you feel and behave in return, is not the most productive environment to be in.

> *If you always do what you've always done, you will always get what you've always got*

Often, we become so entrenched in a particular way of acting, usually as a result of past experiences, that it's difficult to break out of it. But these behaviours keep us stuck in our current situation – so break out of it we must, as this is the only way we will have access to a new beginning, a new life, full of surprises. As they say, "If you always do what you've always done, you will always get what you've always got."

Now is your chance to turn over a new leaf, to try a different approach to achieving a fulfilling life. So instead of muddling through, reacting to events as they happen to you, it's time to *act*, to consciously and actively choose your future. As we said in Chapter Five, even not making a decision is a decision, and again here it's true – you can decide to either embrace or avoid certain influences, depending on whether they are positive or negative. Having studied Neuro-Linguistic Programming (NLP) for years, I'm reluctant to spend too long focusing on negativity, however. Instead, I want you to recognise what no longer works for you, but rather than play the blame game or feel guilty or angry, I just want you to reframe your perspective, and focus only on what you can do about it. Shifting your perspective like this is incredibly liberating – and sometimes it takes hardly any effort at all: it's just a mental decision not to think like that, or continue that habit any more. Try it for yourself.

Now I'm going to discuss a few areas of life where road-blocks on your path to happiness can often occur. Do any of these apply to you, and if so, how can you change your perspective?

The Internet – an instant community, but is it real?

As mentioned in the previous chapter, the internet is an amazing resource – there's a whole world at our fingertips that has never been as accessible as it is now. We can contact people who are thousands of miles away with the click of a mouse. In this absorbing, mesmerising realm, it's easy to forget that it's also a hall of mirrors. Things are not as they seem. Take the example of internet dating. Just as you would endeavour to put the most flattering picture of yourself up on your profile, so people only present a one-dimensional image of themselves too. Who would post a photo of themselves taken on a Sunday morning with bedhead hair and puffy eyes? We want to show our best side to the world and hide our faults, but when an email or a photo is all you've got to go on, how can you know what is real?

In the same way, it is my belief that even after hours or days of emails and online chats, you can never truly know someone until you meet them in real life. Everything else is a façade. By having eye contact, seeing their body language, whether they're relaxed and 'off-guard' or tense and anxious, their tone of voice etc., we get valuable information about the person, often that they're not aware they're communicating. You can use the tips way back in Chapter One about body language to tell you all you need to know about the 'real' person. None of this can be gleaned from virtual relationships online.

Dating websites seem like a sweet shop full of goodies, but did you know that some of the profiles are fake? They've been created by the website to entice people to sign up – those gorgeous creatures with the come-to-bed eyes don't exist in reality. In other areas of social media, the same tricks are being played. For example, some bloggers (not me, I hasten to add) are just in it to make money. They don't really care about the products they rave about, they only care about the traffic to their site and the consequent advertising revenue.

One of the behemoths of the internet, Facebook, can be as toxic as it is enjoyable. It's wonderful to get a glimpse of how 'friends' are getting on, but again, don't be mistaken in thinking that this is an accurate representation of real life. It would be easy to feel discouraged and despondent when everyone around you is in a perpetual state of bliss, raising a glass of champagne in the sunset. In reality, we're all faced with the daily slog of life. Because of my global nomadic lifestyle and my mixed marriage, my Facebook page has an international outreach and is a real joy for me, because I've found out about so many amazing people through it, but I don't consider that I've got to know them: it's only when I meet up with someone face-to-face and engage with them that I can gauge whether they could become a true friend.

Cultural or faith differences – mind the gap

Having had personal experience of this as both the product of my parents' intercultural marriage, and then having a Danish husband myself, I can tell you that as well as the pros, there are cons to bear in mind too. First the pros. Marrying Anders has made me much more open-minded; I have adopted some of his more liberal views and become more Scandinavian in my outlook. I've also become culturally richer because I've gained a whole new experience of life – Scandinavian history, food, traditions. It also turns out that a Singapore/Danish mix makes beautiful children! Okay, that's just my mother's pride talking. Unfortunately there is a downside, which is that there can be a lot of pressure and stress put on an intercultural marriage because of miscommunication problems – a lot can be misconstrued if there is a language barrier and it can be frustrating not to be able to articulate exactly what you mean. Also, divorce rates are very high because people enter the relationship hoping to find happiness and instead have unmet expectations as they hadn't explicitly outlined what their needs were at the beginning. This could happen in any relationship, of course, but in intercultural ones it is even more likely because of the different life experiences and cultural views. I have made sure that despite communicating in both our second languages, Anders and I are always on the same page.

    I know someone from Singapore who is married to a Nigerian man. Culturally they are chalk and cheese.

In particular, his conversational style is loud and full of expansive gesticulation which she finds quite wearing, but also his perception of time is very different to hers. At first his relaxed attitude to punctuality was amusing, but after a time it began to grate on her and she would say: "Don't be so African," which was insulting to him, and also to their children, who bridge the gap between their cultures. Whilst this is quite a minor obstacle to happiness, if too many of them stack up, then the relationship is in trouble.

The cultural differences that make your partner so interesting can also make them irritating when they fail to appreciate your 'charming' cultural occasions. The way Anders and I cope is to allow each other time out during family gatherings or other intense cultural occasions. For example, when he comes to Singapore with me, during big family get-togethers that even I can find quite overwhelming, he knows it's fine by me if he wants to retreat into the bedroom with a book. He doesn't have to be there physically for me to know we are still a strong partnership. Equally, I recently had to return for three months to look after my mother, and he understands that this is expected of me. He doesn't like that I'm away from home, but he respects this caring aspect of my personality. In fact, I'd go so far as to say that my good example has made him closer to his own family.

Anders' late father initially saw me as a traditional Asian bride and would comment about how kind I was, waiting on him hand and foot. We shared a running joke about me patiently peeling his prawns, but as the years went by, my father-in-law realised that my marriage to his son was way more nuanced than this stereotype and that I am a person in my own right, with my own aspirations. He came to respect and admire me and my cultural heritage, which he saw reflected in his own grandchildren.

Your cultural identity is also closely linked with food as evidenced with a couple I worked with who had developed problems due to their opposing views on their native cuisines. This initially seems like a rather trivial issue, but the problem goes a lot deeper than you'd think. He was English, she was Malaysian, and she refused to cook him traditional English food because she found it bland and boring. But he was brought up on the likes of roast beef and Yorkshire pudding, and sausage and mash – this was his comfort food – and whilst he enjoyed the spicy, sizzling Malaysian meals she made, he yearned for the occasional simple roast dinner. By not allowing him to indulge, she was not allowing him to be 100% himself, and we all know what happens when one partner has too much control in the relationship…

This brings me on to interfaith relationships, and I'm reminded of Bibi in Chapter Five, who suppressed her Muslim beliefs to please Henk, with disastrous consequences. I'd describe interfaith relationships as a time bomb that urgently needs to be diffused at the first opportunity. Since faith is our deepest foundation, something we rely on in our darkest hours, we have to be prepared for it to have an impact somewhere down the line in our relationship. Everything is shiny and optimistic during the honeymoon period but beware crises, where views become polarised.

> *Interfaith relationships can be like a time bomb that urgently needs to be diffused at the first opportunity*

To cope with faith differences, I'd suggest you start by confronting your own prejudices. Do you have any knee-jerk reactions to your partner's religion or faith? Then open the doors to communication and learn about why their faith is important to them. A successful interfaith relationship is not about imposing your own views on your partner, it's more like the Buddhist symbol of yin and yang – two beautiful paisley shapes that curl around each other, separate yet together, forming a circle.

Toxic parents – keep your distance

If your relationship with your parents is less than happy, be careful not to let this affect your future partnerships. Lack of attention as a child can leave you feeling needy and insecure with a potential mate whilst too much attention from your parents is overwhelming and interfering, preventing you from opening up fully with a partner.

My own relationship with my mother has been rocky and at one point I decided on a 'no contact' period in adulthood when the situation between us was impacting on my own happiness. When I was growing up, my mother was very 'hands on'. She had an opinion about every aspect of my life, sometimes quite negative, and my self-esteem took a real knocking. As I grew up, I learnt to hold her comments at arm's length, but this in itself was tiring. It was like constantly pulling poison darts out of myself. When I married Anders I realised I would have to break away from her as she was harming our relationship with her constant drip-drip-drip of disapproval. My mother's comments made me feel indignant because she had been single for most of her life – so who was she to dish out relationship advice?

Because of this, I stopped being in contact with her, but as I am Asian, this was a huge decision. Filial piety, or respect for your parents, is one of the mainstays of

Asian culture, and my mother made sure I knew that by hammering it home from an early age. It was hard, but I didn't have any contact with her for two years and it was very painful for both of us – but it was the only way that I could help her to realise that her opinions, which she thought were well meaning, were actually destructive. Gradually she realised that she had been overbearing and apologised to me. We both cried and together we built a new relationship, where she modified her comments and in return I tried to phrase my reactions to them more gently, so neither of us felt hurt.

If you can relate to this, ask yourself: "are my parents' opinions important to me?" Also, vitally, "are they right for me?" No one but you can know whether their advice works for you. As a child, your parent's word is law, and you seek their approval all the time, but as an adult, you can decide if they're a positive or negative influence. Just like the previous chapter about your environment and surrounding yourself with people who nourish and encourage you, if your parents don't fit this category, extricate yourself.

In-laws – how to handle them
In much the same way as toxic parents, in-laws can also be a pain. No one is ever good enough for their darling daughter or son and never will be. Faced with this scenario, a calm head is required. First, you have to see their perspective and understand that this overprotectiveness comes from a loving place. Second, you need to put your foot down with your partner, explaining that they need to stand up to their parents and not allow them to criticise you. It's a delicate area – you want to be polite and friendly to your in-laws but you mustn't sacrifice your own sanity or self-respect.

Two friends, Rose and Andrew found themselves

in this situation. Rose was a nursery teacher and Andrew a management consultant. In his mother's eyes, Rose was not good enough, and her mother-in-law constantly asked Rose if she had considered retraining for a more high-status job. She also made other jibes about her background and her appearance, always when Andrew was out of earshot, so that Rose felt inadequate and began to question whether Andrew secretly shared his mother's views. Of course Andrew didn't, he loved and respected Rose but he reverted to child-mode around his mother to keep the peace.

After a particularly painful visit, Rose declared that she wouldn't be going back there again and if Andrew wanted to see his mother, he could do so on his own. This was difficult for Andrew as his loyalties were torn between the two of them but ultimately he knew that his mother's behaviour was unacceptable and Rose shouldn't be expected to tolerate it. When his mother realised that Rose wasn't coming again, she felt relieved. She wasn't emotionally sophisticated enough to feel ashamed but at least she couldn't inflict her negativity on Rose any more.

Since your partner's parents are very important to them, it's crucial not to be critical of them, regardless of how horrendous they are to you. You must just firmly state what you are not willing to put up with, without getting personal, and stick to your guns.

Ex-partners – get closure

Many people don't have a clean break from their ex-partners and this ends up as baggage in the new relationship. Even though they're strictly not together any more, their ex still has influence over their behaviour and can compromise the happiness of the current relationship. I used to have a boyfriend whose ex insisted on using him as her support network. Her mother was terminally ill, and because my boyfriend had met her, his ex felt that he understood the situation better than anyone and therefore was the best person to provide sympathy for her.

As her mum's condition deteriorated, the phone calls became more and more frequent until it felt like she was a constant presence in our relationship. She took to calling round and she co-opted my boyfriend into discussions about the situation, often into the early hours. As they were both Dutch, I couldn't understand their conversations, which made me feel even more excluded. I would make myself scarce when she arrived, as I was aware that she wanted some privacy with him, and this went on for many months, until one day I stopped and thought: "Hang on a moment! You're coming into my house and monopolising my boyfriend!" I do believe it's possible to have platonic friendships between men and women but there are limits and this woman was definitely imposing on our relationship. Your partner should be your priority and whilst, of course, it's natural and healthy to have other friendships, they should not be at the expense of your primary relationship.

I put my foot down and said to my boyfriend that it was time for her to find another shoulder to cry on. He accepted this and the intensity of their friendship subsided until she became just another person in our social circle again. Unfortunately, my partner went on to cheat on me with another woman who demanded his attention because she was lonely, so his desire to make other women happy was always going to take precedence over my feelings. In retrospect, I can see that his behaviour with the grieving woman should have been a red flag for me, but unfortunately I didn't realise it at the time. Hindsight is a wonderful thing.

Happily, he is firmly in my 'ex' department, and there is no chance of him influencing my current relationship! Shared experiences with an ex will always give you that intimate connection, but resist the temptation to stay in touch because of it. There was a reason you broke up, and keep that at the forefront of your mind.

Children – remember their needs

A very difficult road-block that requires a lot of careful manoeuvring to negotiate is when either you or a potential partner has children. Stepchildren can be a wonderful addition to your life but they can also bring challenges. For example, if you meet someone who has a difficult relationship with their ex, then the children can be caught in the middle and used as pawns in the battle. The hostility between the adults can affect how the ex feels about you, and whether they are happy to allow you to be around their children. Your parenting style may conflict with theirs too, or they may feel unhappy about you disciplining them. It's a minefield, so tread carefully.

One couple I know discovered the difficulties of step-parenting when the man introduced his two daughters to his new partner. She is a very straightforward, no-nonsense type of woman and when she saw how spoilt and unboundaried his children were, it made her think twice about having children with him herself. It was an awkward situation to be in, because she also felt unable to discipline his children in the way she would have if they were her own. Children are of course a joy, but they can also be fire-starters, playing the parents off against each other: "Muuumeeee, Daddy said I could have…"

Another woman I know had a boyfriend who disliked her daughter. The grandparents of this girl had custody, so the mum only saw her at weekends, but the new boyfriend refused to spend any time with the girl, and so as a consequence, the mother began spending less time with her daughter too. It's unusual for a woman to sacrifice her daughter's happiness for her own, but I don't judge her because whatever works for her is her prerogative though she has to be willing to cope with the repercussions from her daughter in later life.

In a more cheery scenario, another family I know get along so well with each other's exes that they all go on holiday together! Not only does it save them money, but it's also practical – they can enjoy each other's company and also have built-in babysitters for one-to-one couples' time. Win-win!

It's essential to discuss the issue of children deeply before you move forward in the relationship. Ask each other (and yourself) do you want to be a role model for his/her children? Equally, is your partner someone you would want your children to be influenced by? Also, how will the children react to being in a blended family? This will need a lot of preparation, discussion and time before things run smoothly.

> *Do you want children together? You need to be absolutely certain that you're on the same page here*

The second big issue is whether you want children together. You need to be absolutely certain that you're on the same page here, because children have a massive impact on your life that you really can't appreciate until they're born. Sit down together and discuss openly whether you want children or not. If so, how many children do each of you feel makes an ideal family and also what is your parenting style? If one of you wants children and the other doesn't, then this can be the biggest road-block of all. There's not really any place you can go from here other than apart. Compromise on this one issue, more than any, will be the road to disaster. Sad though it may be, if you cannot agree on the issue of children, then it is time to go your separate ways.

Childlessness can also be a bit of a minefield, even if it is a mutual decision in the relationship. Women who have children often pity those who do not, feeling that they are missing out, or worse, not normal. Several childless women I know have actually suffered from bullying by their well-meaning but condescending friends, who try to persuade them to change their minds. We are getting into the realm of toxic relationships here, so if you are comfortable with your decision, then you need to vocalise this to your friends and family. Parents and in-laws can also pressurise the childless couple because of their desire to have grandchildren. It takes strength to have the courage of your convictions, so don't be swayed by those who think they know what's best for you.

If and when you are blessed with children, you also need to safeguard your relationship in preparation for their arrival. I remember just before my eldest daughter was born, I was watching Dr Phil on Oprah and he said that children did not ask to come into your life but now they're here, they're going on your journey, so you shouldn't change your relationship for them. I've never forgotten that. Always remember that you were first a loving partner before you were a parent. I do feel this is more of a 'mum problem' – when you're exhausted with a new-born, the temptation to wear tents and stop making an effort is huge but try to remember you have your own identity as well as that of a mother.

Mental health problems – a personal issue

Sadly, a friend's partner committed suicide last year – she had been depressed for many years – and her partner was racked with guilt because he felt to blame. I told him that unfortunately there was nothing more he could have done, and that sometimes people are drawn to us because they think we can help them, when in reality, we can only help ourselves. Nonetheless, he still felt guilt stricken. He'd had previous girlfriends who suffered with low mood and he thought it may have been his fault somehow. I gently suggested that rather than blame himself, perhaps he needed to look at why he chose people who were needy or damaged in some way. It made me wonder what it was that he was avoiding looking at in himself.

With mental health issues there is no quick fix and although you may see a brief respite when you first get together, the cloud of potential relapse is a permanent fixture on the horizon. It would be nice if love alone was enough to guide them out of that dark place but I'm afraid it isn't. Change and recovery is only possible from within, it cannot be initiated by a partner, so if you meet someone with problems, and here I'm including addiction, your best bet is to encourage them to seek help, rather than get any closer.

I had two friends who struggled with this thorny issue. Emma had been waiting for years for Jack to propose but he was reluctant to as she was a very heavy drinker and smoker. He came to me wanting me to 'fix' her. As a therapist, I explained that could only happen if she approached me herself. Years later Emma did decide to come herself and she poured her heart out to me. She'd had an unhappy childhood and she used alcohol and tobacco as crutches. She felt that because Jack didn't want to marry her, he was withholding love, which was very painful for her, making her rely more heavily on the drugs. Together we realised that the only way she could break out of this vicious circle was to tackle the root of the problem, her low self-esteem due to her abusive parents. Emma decided to go to therapy and managed to stop smoking and to just drink socially. Emma and Jack's relationship has gone from strength to strength since she made this life-changing and very courageous decision. He still hasn't popped the question but Emma no longer fixates on that as being symbolic of his love. Jack has become very loving and she is secure enough in herself to know that they are happy together regardless.

Long-distance relationships – get your priorities straight

When you live away from your partner, it's usually due to your career, which suggests that you place a lot of importance on it. When I see career-centric couples it makes me wonder what their priorities are since neither is willing to compromise or relocate for the other. It's a glamorous lifestyle – imagine a high-flying lawyer in Hong Kong jetting over to see her banker boyfriend in Korea every weekend – you only see the best side of your partner and never have to discuss the minutiae of living together, like whose turn it is to change the sheets. It may be that when you finally do cohabit you discover that he's a slob or she spends hours gossiping on the phone and the sparkle goes out of the relationship when you realise that they're not the person you thought they were.

For a long-distance relationship to sustain long-term, your trust in each other has to be rock-solid. Talking on the phone and via Skype is no substitute for face-to-face contact (although I do know a couple who enjoy Skype sex!) and you can feel isolated midweek. The other necessity is for both parties to have similar personalities – yes career-driven, but also independent and with no children, because when one person is left doing all the childcare, resentment can build.

I gave up my career to become the trailing spouse, following Anders around the world. It was something I was prepared to do because being together was more important to me than my professional life, although it didn't take me long to reinvent my career to allow family life to flourish. But if there is no chance of relocating, for example, if your job is site-specific, then you need to come up with creative solutions to cope. Once again, if this looks like it may become your situation, sit down together and talk, don't rely on those feel-good hormones that are buzzing around at the beginning of a relationship to sustain you in the following lonely weeks and months.

Love on the rebound – take it gently

If you've come out of a relationship that's left you feeling battered and bruised, you need caring for and nurturing back to good (mental) health. This is when a rebound relationship comes in. It fulfils the needs of that particular moment but isn't necessarily the right relationship for you for the rest of your life. An analogy is that, if you're in hospital, you're bandaged and given medicine by a caring nurse but you don't fall in love with them. In the same way, on the rebound, you may be getting the attention you crave after months of neglect and even harm from the old, toxic relationship, but don't forget to ask yourself whether you actually like *them*, or just the pampering they're giving you.

As I mentioned in Chapter Four about sexuality, I had a rebound relationship with someone who restored my self-esteem after an abusive relationship. He wasn't someone who I could be with long-term as whilst I appreciated his healing words, I didn't feel strongly enough about him as a person. I had been hungry for so long that I became greedy for his devotion. It was only when I had recovered that I realised he wasn't the man I had in my head, the one I had visualised (that was lucky old Anders).

If you have recently emerged from a long-term relationship, give yourself the chance to remember who you are as a person – go out and have some crazy nights, flirt, be silly, relax and look around at everyone there is who could be potential partners. To use my favourite architectural analogy once again, if you've been living in an old shack for years, don't make your new home the nearest static caravan – consider a mansion, a thatched cottage or a duplex before you decide what's right for you.

Age gaps – a bridge too far?
May-to-December relationships are generally thought to be between an older man and a younger woman but the rise of the 'cougar' (women who date younger men) means that it can now go either way, and of course age gaps can be just as tricky in same-sex relationships too. My thoughts are that unless you are talking about a small gap, such as seven years or less, there are more cons than pros. Being born in different decades means you have different tastes in music, fashion, culture and even attitudes to life. Compare the 70s to the 80s for instance – such contrasting times and influences. You look at things completely differently

and the number of years under your belt can change your approach vastly.

Take travelling, for example. The younger partner may be enthusiastic and full of excitement about seeing the world and want to go off backpacking whilst the older party is jaded, with a 'been there, done that' attitude and would be happier with a city break. This would be frustrating for the youngster and irritating for the oldie. A gay couple I know found that holidays were their flashpoint. The youngster yearned to sample the nightlife whilst the older man preferred a sedate meal and a stroll on the seafront. Their energy levels didn't mesh well either – guess who wanted to rush around exhibitions and who wanted to laze on the beach?

> *What can at first seem charming can become the source of friction as the differences between you become magnified over the years*

As with the inter-cultural relationships, what can at first seem charming can become the source of friction as the differences between you become magnified over the years. The question is, can you cope with this? If your solution is to also spend time with friends whose likes and dislikes chime more with your own than your partner, ask yourself if you wouldn't be happier with someone more compatible? As usual, I prescribe lots of conversations before the relationship becomes serious, and some deep thinking on your own too.

Attitudes to money – be on the same page

One of my motivations for writing this book is so that I am working towards becoming financially independent. It's important to me as a mum that my children see that women can be independent and have responsible attitudes towards money, and it's important for Anders to know that I am endeavouring to contribute financially towards our lives. We joke about me becoming the breadwinner whilst he stays at home drumming but I don't see why I shouldn't try to make that dream a reality. (Although many dads will soon find out that a stay-at-home mum's life isn't as easy as it looks.)

Happily, we have similar attitudes to money. We learnt this during financial coaching with a mentor who made sure we were on the right track. Within two months of being together, we were pooling our incomes in the same bank account. We have nothing to hide and as Anders earns much more than I do, he trusts me not to overspend. I am the bargain-bin queen when it comes to clothes and household goods, and I don't mind anyone knowing, and Anders doesn't have any lavish outlays either. If I hear about someone who has a secret bank account because of their partner's spendthrift ways, I feel alarmed. Why can't they discuss it and come to a compromise? Also, what else is being hidden?

Having the same expectations and working methods is the key to a harmonious financial relationship. A friend of mine has a husband who is always looking for a way to make a fast buck, whilst she works full-time in a steady job. His finances are all over the place whilst hers are constant and predictable. She is encouraging and supportive to him but privately said to me that she finds trying to rustle up enthusiasm for the next 'big deal' tiring and would much prefer him to work in a conventional job. This sad confession made me wonder how much longer their marriage can cope with this tension. Neither one's attitude to money is superior, they're just mismatched.

As I've said before, honesty is crucial – from knowing how much s/he earns to how you feel about their spending. If it jars with you at the beginning, then it certainly won't improve.

Partners who are otherwise attached – forbidden territory
I have been the 'other woman' twice in my life – both times without my knowledge, I hasten to add. Both men omitted to tell me that they were married: one time, I found out during our relationship and I ended it; the other time I found out after we'd split up. I felt awful when I discovered the truth. One of them even had a wife who was pregnant at the time, which is just horrendous and so cruel.

I believe that if you're with someone who is already in a relationship, then they're not with you for the right reason. If they're juggling another love interest, then they're not disengaging with that person and engaging fully with you. What does that say about your self-esteem? Are you not worthy of someone who is 100% yours? By accepting second best, you're denying yourself happiness.

I knew someone who was dating a married man and he constantly repeated that old chestnut: "My wife doesn't understand me." I said to her that that is only his perspective and if you asked the wife, you may discover a whole different story. To know the truth you have to hear it from the horse's mouth, otherwise you'll just be told what she/he thinks you want to hear.

People who are otherwise attached want the excitement of an affair without considering the hurt for everyone involved. It can never be a long-term relationship because thinking about the karma – if she/he's done it *with* you, then what's stopping her/him doing it *to* you? If a relationship is failing, you need to have the guts to walk away from it and spend time single, reflecting on what went wrong, rather than using another person as a reason to split.

When I first met Anders, we were both with other people. The moment I looked at him I knew that we had something special together but because he had a girlfriend he was firmly out of bounds. I thought, "Wow, if only I could meet a single guy like him." My boyfriend at the time had asked me to marry him but I was delaying because I knew he wasn't right for me. After much thought and soul-searching, I broke it off with him and when he asked me if there was anyone else, it felt good to honestly say no.

After our split I kept bumping in to Anders until he finally asked me for a coffee. I said I would only accept if it wasn't for romantic reasons, because he was still attached. He confessed that he was unhappy with his girlfriend and I told him to talk to her and see if there was any way they could resolve their problems – I refused to be the reason for this relationship breakdown. He took my advice, they talked and agreed that the best course of action was to call it a day. The rest, as they say, is history.

Love Is Just Around The Corner

So there you have it – the blueprint for your dream home. You've done all the hard work, the research, the strategy, the discussions and soul-searching. Now I give you (planning) permission to go out there and build it! By following the chapters in this book, you have been preparing yourself, inside and out, for future happiness.

> *Enunciate clearly what you want and you will be rewarded*

In Chapter One, you've learnt how to make the most of yourself physically and have become versed in body language. Chapter Two taught you that your emotional intelligence is now sky high and you know how to genuinely listen, not only to others, but to what you need yourself. Chapter Three covered your intellect, encouraging you to be at ease with yourself whilst making sure you reach for the stars. In Chapter Four, the world of sexuality and sensuality was explored, ensuring that you know exactly what you're comfortable with. Chapter Five found you looking at your sources of spirituality, an essential part of your make-up and Chapter Six made sure you were perfectly positioned in order for love and happiness to flow freely towards you. A hard hat, high-vis jacket and steel-toe-capped boots were provided in Chapter Seven, to make sure that you know where the road-blocks are and how to be careful when you're busy constructing that amazing new home for yourself. The thread running through these chapters, like mortar between the bricks, is the absolutely essential need for communication. Keep those lines open and clear between you and the world: enunciate clearly what you want and you will be rewarded.

> *Through self-discovery, comes wisdom*

Most importantly of all, this book will have taught you about the power of visualisation. As a house is built, brick by brick, so your rosy future was assembled in your mind's eye. Hold on to that vision, keep it close, because it holds the key to the rest of your life. Through self-discovery, comes wisdom.

This book can become your guide – return to it when you start to falter or forget your vision and you will soon be reinvigorated and ready once again. I'm so sure that this book will work for you that I invite you to contact me when it does, letting me know your happy endings. Just drop me a line at www.arnierozahkrogh.com. Who knows? My next book could include your story as inspiration for other hopeful singles.

The 20 Questions Game

In the early weeks of our relationship, Anders and I sat down and asked each other these questions. I'd really recommend you try it when you meet a new partner. It's not only great fun, but it also gives you a glimpse of how compatible you are. You may have got to know your partner 'intimately' but do you know them intimately? If your answers are different, this doesn't signal disaster, just that they're a topic for discussion. You can negotiate, compromise or even agree to disagree, but at least these delicate issues are out on the table early on, instead of rearing their heads later in the relationship, long after the honeymoon is over.

There is that old adage in business – 'If you fail to plan, you plan to fail' and while nobody plans to fail at a relationship, jumping right in without really knowing what you're getting into can be dangerous. These questions help you to discover what makes your new love tick and give you a heads-up about how he/she feels about the big issues in life. This way, you can predict how they might react in future situations.

1. What is your favourite colour and how does it make you feel?
   (You'll never buy the wrong colour scarf or socks for your partner again.)
2. What is your favourite cuisine and why?
   (A Valentine's Day surprise meal will always be in the right restaurant.)
3. Who was your favourite teacher growing up and why?
   (This will tell you what personality traits your partner admires.)
4. What was one of your best memories growing up?
   (Good memories sometimes help one to firm up their moral values

and gives you an insight into what made them happy in the past)

5. Who was your childhood role model?
   ((This help explains what they find to be characteristics they admire and can explain why they are obsessed about that sports star or that female actress)

6. What was the best lesson someone taught you?
   (This helps you see if they're the type to remember powerful words or deeds and if they'll remember the conversation you have today, tomorrow)

7. Did you have a good relationship with your grandparents?
   ((Unlike parents, grandparents love and care for us in a different way. This also helps you to see if they are the patient type and enjoy companies of people of different age groups and generations)

8. Did you enjoy playing with your younger siblings and cousins?
   (In case you have an inkling that you might like kids in the future, this conversation might be easier if you know they have paternal/maternal feelings)

9. What kind of sports do you like watching and which do you enjoy playing?
   (Most people appreciate it when you show interest in their favourite sports/teams. Maybe a great surprise gift for the future?)

10. What kind of books/magazines do you like to read and why?
    (Gives you an insight into your cultural compatibility.)

11. What kind of music do you like to listen to for relaxing/energising/cleaning?
    (Again, it will allow you to assess whether you have similar cultural tastes and if you can compromise)

12. What is your idea of a blissful holiday?
    (Don't want to be caught out arguing about city or beach

destinations in the future, do we? Holidays can bring back great memories and give the person a loving glow just by sharing)

13. Where do you see yourself retiring one day?
    (Do you envisage a similar future and if not, what compromises might need to be made?)

14. Which country do you think is your twin and why?
    (Refer to the 'Emotional Types' in Chapter Two, and assess your compatibility!)

15. Are you for or against capital punishment?
    (This could be a deal breaker if you disagree as morality issues can make one passionate.)

16. Could you survive on a desert island alone with just a Swiss Army knife, some string, a tarpaulin and a flint?
    (You might like to choose your Desert Island Discs and favourite book too.)

17. If you knew you had three days left to live, what would you do?
    (A sobering but insightful look at what you really think is important in life.)

18. If you won millions in the lottery next week, what would you do?
    (This will tell you what your core values are – altruistic or adventurous, cautious or crazy!)

19. If you could wake up one day with a new skill, what would it be?
    (Whether it's an ability to paint or swim the channel, this question gives you an understanding of your partner's aspirations.)

20. Did you have a pet growing up and what was its name?
    (Pets tend to lead towards empathy in humans. If your partner had a pet, they're quite like to be natural caring and nurturing.)

Bibliography

Chapter One

1. Willis, Janine and Todorov, Alexander. Psychological Science July 2006 vol. 17.
2. http://huff.to/2jmmAnB
3. Hamermesh, Daniel. Beauty Pays: Why Attractive People are More Successful. Princeton University Press.
4. http://bit.ly/2kdwjuH
5. http://bit.ly/1np5QGi
6. Mehrabian, A., & Blum, J. S. (1997). Physical appearance, attractiveness, and the mediating role of emotions. Current Psychology, vol. 16, 20-42.
7. Darwin, Charles. The Expression of the Emotions in Man and Animals. New York: D. Appleton and Company (1872).
8. http://bit.ly/1oxz0pU
9. Gueguen, Nicolas and Fischer-Lokou, Jacques. Another evaluation of touch and helping behaviour. Psychological Reports, 2003, 92, 62-64.
10. Pease, Allan and Barbara, The Definitive Book of Body Language. Orion.
11. http://bit.ly/2jN2tO0
12. http://huff.to/1KfZu5L

Chapter Two

13. Geher, Glenn. Perceived and Actual Characteristics of Parents and Partners: A Test of a Freudian Model of Mate Selection. Current Psychology (Fall, 2000), vol. 19, no.3, 194-214.

14. http://bit.ly/2kdAdns
15. http://bit.ly/2j0yQeF
16. Goleman, D. Emotional Intelligence: Why it can matter more than IQ. Bantam Books.
17. http://bit.ly/2jsUUuy
18. http://pewrsr.ch/2knsZQO
19. Wiseman, Richard. 59 Seconds: Think a Little, Change a Lot. Pan.
20. http://bit.ly/1ueqZYe
21. http://bit.ly/2kduVbE

Chapter Three

22. http://bit.ly/2jV3V2M
23. http://bit.ly/1qTm018
24. http://bit.ly/2jaA3LS
25. http://nyti.ms/2kpp9CI
26. http://bit.ly/2kerYHL
27. http://bit.ly/2jZ3Jji
28. http://bit.ly/2j1ieUm

Chapter Four

29. http://bit.ly/2ksDr9P
30. http://bit.ly/2k3kdab
31. http://bit.ly/2jZuNhV
32. http://bit.ly/2jptR66
33. de Bono, Edward. How to have a Beautiful Mind. Vermillion.
34. http://bit.ly/2ksuCgi
35. http://bit.ly/QdAhCU
36. http://wb.md/2jeAhl0
37. http://researchnews.osu.edu/archive/sexthoughts.htm

38. http://bit.ly/2kmxZ5e
39. http://bit.ly/2jUv04a
40. http://bit.ly/2jxgr5C

Chapter Five

41. The Bible. Matthew 7:24-27, New International Version (NIV)
42. http://bit.ly/2jsRjPI
43. http://bzfd.it/2jiwzH9
44. Ian Dury and The Blockheads, Reasons to be Cheerful, Part 3, http://bit.ly/1zTA87V
45. http://richardlouv.com
46. http://bit.ly/2j7Vdz7
47. Khalil Gibran, The Prophet. BN Publishing

Chapter Six

48. http://read.bi/17ZcXm5
49. http://bit.ly/2k8XoBR
50. http://on.today.com/2kA99hg
51. Chopra, Deepak. Creating Affluence: The A-to-Z Steps to a Richer Life. New World Library
52. http://bit.ly/2k8U8pZ
53. http://bit.ly/2kaonx4
54. http://huff.to/1yLbpIi
55. http://bit.ly/2kAlGWq
56. Burkeman, Oliver. This Column Will Change Your Life, The Guardian, 21.11.16

ABOUT THE AUTHOR

She was born in Singapore into a mixed family, raised by her grandparents while her single mum juggled 3 jobs to feed 4 kids and 2 elderly parents. When her mum was matched made to marry again, when Ar'nie was 10, and that marriage failed shortly after, she became interested in psychology and relationships. The first book she picked up on human relationship at that age was the acclaimed Dale Carnegie's "How to Win Friends and Influence People".

When asked at primary school what she wanted to do when older, she said a doctor, so she can 'inject' people with happiness and take away their pain. Today she tries to inject happiness through her coaching and therapy work and the volunteering she does.

She also loves cooking up a storm in the kitchen and feeding 'happiness' to family and friends. When she's not at home with her 4 kids, she is out with her husband laughing away at comedy shows, dancing away at live music gigs or getting muddy, camping at music festivals (her favourite is Glastonbury!).

Interested in her coaching session or a workshop or having her speak at your event? Get in touch via *www.ArnieRozahKrogh.com.*

Photograph by Amelia Zara Krogh

Printed in Great Britain
by Amazon